Tempus ORAL HISTORY SERIES

Southend
voices

Tempus ORAL HISTORY *Series*

Southend
voices

Frances Clamp

TEMPUS

Frontispiece: *Southend pier in the early years of the twentieth century.*

First published 2004

Tempus Publishing Limited
The Mill, Brimscombe Port,
Stroud, Gloucestershire, GL5 2QG

www.tempus-publishing.com

British Library Cataloguing in Publication Data.
A catalogue record for this book is available from the British Library.

ISBN 0 7524 3215 X

Typesetting and origination by Tempus Publishing Limited
Printed in Great Britain by Midway Colour Print, Wiltshire

Contents

Foreword

As a former councillor and mayor of Southend-on-Sea I have come to love and appreciate the many different sides of this fascinating town. Many people believe that the seafront is all there is to Southend. How wrong they are! There are first-rate operatic societies, orchestras, drama groups and parks that are second to none in the country.

Apart from that, Southend is at the centre of a huge amount of work done for charity and there is still a very vibrant seafront. Some of the old landmarks have disappeared, including the beautiful Edwardian bandstand and most of the Kursaal. However, others, like Porters, the ancient priory and most of the pier, remain. There are also some interesting new buildings.

Although the mayor chairs the council, his role is very much a social one. During my mayoral year I learnt far more about the town than I had previously known and I was also privileged to meet many people from all walks of life. They are the lifeblood of the town. In a book of this type it is also possible to meet a great diversity of people, as they share their many and varied memories of Southend-on-Sea through the written word. These memories could so easily be lost, but within these pages we can relive the past. Memories of Southend are well worth preserving. It is a town of which we can be justly proud.

Geoffrey Ayre
(Mayor of Southend-on-Sea, 1991–1992)

Introduction

Per Mare Per Ecclesiam – 'By the Sea and By the Church'. This is the motto of Southend-on-Sea and it reflects two great influences on the development of the town. To many, Southend is simply a trippers' paradise, full of noise, candyfloss and slot machines. Yet to those of us who know and love the town it is far more.

I was born and grew up in Southend before moving to Brentwood after my marriage and the birth of my children, yet I remain a Southendian at heart. However, when I was first asked to write this book I felt rather apprehensive. Did I still have enough contacts to create a worthwhile piece of work? I arranged my first interviews and set off with a small tape recorder, spare batteries and a list of chapter headings.

Although most people told me they didn't have anything interesting to say, from the moment they started talking it was obvious how wrong they were. I believed that I knew the town, yet each new contributor opened windows on events about which I knew little or nothing. There were glimpses of life during both the wars of the twentieth century. I discovered more about the shops and the multitude of leisure activities in the town. Yet the importance of the sea and the church always came through.

The Southend coat of arms neatly sums up the town's history, as a fisherman and a Cluniac monk are shown. Prittlewell lies to the north of modern-day Southend. In the Middle Ages it had a thriving priory at the bottom of the hill and the church of St Mary the Virgin at the top. Just a few fishing cottages existed at the south end of the village by the sea, close to where the Kursaal now stands. Further along the coast to the west was Leigh, a flourishing fishing village with St Clement's church on the hill above. To the east was Southchurch, with its ancient church of Holy Trinity, and to the north was Eastwood, with its own church dedicated to St Lawrence. The symbols of each of these churches appear on the coat of arms: lilies for St Mary, an anchor for St Clement, a gridiron for St Lawrence and the trefoil for Holy Trinity.

With its seven miles of coast stretching from Leigh to Shoebury, the sea has inevitably played an important part in the development of the town. As it became fashionable to visit the seaside, enterprising entrepreneurs realised that the area could have a future as a bathing resort. A fine hotel was built and a terrace of superior houses at the top of what is now known as Pier Hill. Early in the nineteenth century, Southend received royal patronage when five-year-old Princess Charlotte and her mother Princess Caroline came to visit. The elegant houses where they stayed were renamed Royal Terrace. At that time, some people felt that the town was too quiet!

The tide at Southend goes out a very long way. At first, a wooden jetty was built to help visitors arriving by boat, but this was inadequate. Eventually, an iron pier was opened to the public in 1889 and in the following year it became the first in the country to have an electric tramway. Extensions have been added over the years and Southend now has the longest pleasure pier in the world at 1.33 miles. It played a vital part during the Second World War and has faced various disasters over the years, but it remains the town's best-known landmark.

Southend needed to adapt once more when the railway reached the town in 1856. People from the east of London could now travel to the seaside on day trips. Enterprising Southendians made sure that they catered for the needs of these new visitors. At the same time there was a large increase in the residential population.

In the early years of the twentieth century, Southend continued to flourish as a seaside town. However, in the post-war period an increasing number of people began to take their holidays abroad. It was time for the town to find a new identity. Backs were turned on the sea and a vibrant commercial centre developed close to the old village of Prittlewell.

Now the wheel has gone full circle. The pier and its surroundings are once more being restored and a major air show takes place annually over the estuary, helping to attract visitors back to Southend. The town is rediscovering itself yet again.

Southend has always been a town of survivors – people who face setbacks with courage and resourcefulness. During the writing of this book I have been privileged to return once more to the town of my birth to meet some of these people. Each one had a unique story to tell. I only hope that you get the same pleasure from reading their stories as I did in recording them.

Acknowledgements

Special thanks are due to my husband Roger, for all his help and support throughout this project; to Geoffrey Ayre, Sylvia Kent, Nigel Havens, Lois Holmes and Pamela Bissell; to Janet Knowles of Westcliff High School for Girls, David Goody and Michelle Williams from Southend United Football Club; the staff of Southend Borough Council, Southend Library, Ken Crowe and the staff of Southend Museum, The Essex Record Office (Southend Branch) and Echo Newspapers. My thanks too go to everyone who has given so generously of their time to share their memories and treasured photographs. Without them this book would have remained a dream.

Every effort has been made to trace ownership of photographs and to check that the facts given in this book are correct. My apologies for any unwitting errors or omissions.

Frances Clamp, 2003

1 Early Life

Life in an Army hut

We arrived in Southend from the Isle of Wight in 1919 and moved in with my aunt in Southview Drive. I was ten. My father was a pork butcher who had always wanted to be a market gardener. During the First World War he heard about a suitable property in Eastwood Road, now known as Prince Avenue. At that time the house, later called Melrose, hadn't been built.

One of my uncles worked for the Office of Works and he found us an old wooden officer's hut that had been used during the First World War at Southend Aerodrome. This was erected on the Melrose site. We had no furniture, because my mother hadn't been able to bring it from the Isle of Wight. Instead we sat on sugar boxes and used orange boxes for our shoes! The winter that year was very bad. The hut had no services so we moved temporarily into a house on the other side of the road, known as the Pest House. While we were there we all lived in one room.

Our new house was finally ready in 1921-22. I moved in with my parents and my younger brother, Frank. At first we were still without electricity, gas or main drainage. We went to bed with candles, but we did have a cooker – a range in the kitchen.

Rhoda Deane (née Bagnald)

Street games

I played in the street a lot in Surbiton Avenue. One of our favourite games was Tin-Can Copper. One boy turned his back while the rest kicked a can down the road. When the first boy went to find the can the other children hid. Then he had to find the others. If he couldn't find them they could run out and kick the can further away. Another game we played was Knock Down Ginger. That was when we knocked on a door and ran away to hide before anyone came to open it. Most of all I liked playing football in Southchurch Park.

John Horsley

Grandma's house

I lived in Woodside in Leigh when I was small. It backed onto Belfairs Wood so it was like living in the country. The house was called 'Drallig', which was our surname spelt backwards. I thought that was very funny! Later we moved in with my grandma, who lived in 'Sharwood' in Southbourne Grove. It was a lovely house with trees to climb and all sorts of places to explore in the garden. The house is still there, but sadly some of the ground has been sold.

Sally Hall (née Gillard)

Above: *Melrose, the home of the Bagnald family from 1922.*

Below: *Sally Gillard at Keddies, c. 1947.*

Too young for school!

My first memory of Chalkwell School was in 1929 when I was four. We were living in Fairfax Drive at that time. One lunchtime I was playing with a boy who was about six months older than me, and after a few minutes he told me that he had to go back to school. I decided to go too, so I walked all the way to Chalkwell School, which involved crossing one major road all by myself. I went into the infants school, where the headmistress was a delightful lady called Miss Mann. The teacher of the 'babies' class took me to the headmistress who asked me where my mother was. She said I could sit in the classroom with the other children until she found my older brother. In the meantime I was given a slate, a rubber and a stick of chalk until my brother took me home.

When I returned six months later to enrol properly at the school, Miss Mann remembered our earlier encounter, but by then I had my mother with me so everything was fine.

Frank Dudley

The circus comes to town

It must have been around 1914 and there were few houses beyond Wellington Avenue in those days. I remember once sitting on a farm gate at the top of Eastwood Road, near Southbourne Grove, and looking down the field towards Prittlewell Brook over the top of canvas screens. These were set around a visiting circus. I was thrilled at the sight of galloping horses ridden by yelling cowboys and whooping Indians.

Arthur Hance

Trays of teeth

My father was a dental technician. Sometimes, when I was very small, I visited his workshop and one of my favourite pastimes was to sort out the false teeth. These were kept in shallow drawers and were carefully arranged by size and colour. That wasn't my method and the apprentices thought it was very funny to see the way I painstakingly messed up the whole system.

Pamela Livingston

Nearly a kidnap!

The family always say that I ran away to London at the age of three and a half! What actually happened was that my father, who was a fisherman, was working a boat out of Hole

Arthur Hance, kneeling on the far right, was head boy of London Road School in around 1920.

Haven, on the other side of Canvey Island. I heard my mother say that father would be coming home on the train so I decided to walk from where we lived in Glendale Gardens down to the old town to meet him.

In the summer of 1932 there was a level crossing over the railway line. Somehow I managed to get between the level-crossing gates and onto the platform. A train came into the station and I leant from the platform to the side of the carriage. At that moment a portly gentleman picked me up by my knickers and pushed me into the carriage. He got in behind me and shut the door.

Some time later there was an argument with a lady asking if I had a ticket. Of course I hadn't. We got as far as Upminster when I was put in the charge of the porter who got me a bar of chocolate. The next day my mother had to take me to the police station because they were convinced that I had been kidnapped!

Elvina Savill (née Osborne)

Elvina Savill in 2003.

The pit

The Roots Hall football ground is built on the site of an old sandpit, but the sand was excavated in the 1930s. As a small boy I used to play there. Dozens of empty petrol cans were scattered around – they must originally have held around 50 gallons each. They became goalposts for our football games.

As 5 November approached each year we built a magnificent bonfire on the site. It took a month to make until it finally became as high as a house. In those days what is now Roots Hall Avenue was called Gossett Avenue, named after a local councillor. The people who lived there were likely to light the fire in advance, so we left guards to make sure that the Guy Fawkes celebrations didn't start early! There was great rivalry between the Gossett Avenue residents and those from nearby roads.

Frank Dudley

Call-up papers

I went to a little nursery school in a house on the corner of Danescroft Drive and Elmsleigh Drive. There was a small hall there, but it has been pulled down now.

One of my most vivid memories is of my mother standing in the dining room crying. I was three then. Daddy came in and picked me up. He gave me a hug and a kiss and said, 'Look after mummy.' He had just received his call-up papers.

Lois Holmes (née Hance)

Services at the bandstand

My grandparents lived in Lime Avenue and we visited them regularly when I was small – often we stayed for two weeks at a time. We used to go to church services at the bandstand

David Wigley with his sister Elisabeth at Leigh Paddling Pool, c. 1965.

adapted classical music to suit our dances. When we were about five we wore pastel Greek-style dresses with two pleats at the front and back. There were slits up the sides and a girdle with tassels that must not hang below the dress. If we were cold we wore little angora boleros, the same colour as our dresses. All the dresses were made by Miss Bellairs, and Miss Layborn inspected them the first time we wore them. We learned many different dances, including one with silver-painted Indian clubs. Woe betide you if you dropped a club!

Sally Hall

A plane comes down and scarlet fever strikes

My first real memory was of a plane coming down in the field behind our house in Cromwell Road, where Eastern Avenue now runs, on the far side of the Victory Sports Ground. This was during the First World War, so I was quite young.

When I was four I had scarlet fever and had to go into the Balmoral Road Fever Hospital. It was a notifiable disease and the doctor recommended that I went there. Otherwise my mother would have had to cut herself off from all other human contact.

I was away from home for six weeks, but I do remember two things from my stay. Firstly, I had only one bath during all that time. There was a real Victorian nurse looking after me. As she prepared the water she put in a thermometer, something I hadn't seen before. I asked what it was. 'Don't be inquisitive!' she snapped. That was a typical attitude towards children in those days.

My second memory is of visiting time. Parents were only allowed to visit for an hour on Sunday afternoons. They spoke to the patient through a window. Apparently my mother asked me at what time I went to bed.

on Sunday mornings in the summer. Cliff Town congregational church took over the bandstand at those times.

I loved visiting the old swimming pool at Leigh. It was on the edge of the beach and filled up with water at every high tide. There were lots of crabs in the walls.

Sometimes we went into Old Leigh, where a bridge crossed over the road. On one occasion we bought some cockles and mussels from the cockle sheds but I turned my nose up at them!

David Wigley

Miss Layborn's ballet classes

Miss Audrey Layborn was my ballet teacher. She was very much of the old school – an elegant lady, very strict but greatly respected. Miss Hilliard played the grand piano and

13

The Girls' Life Brigade band with Lois Hance first left in the front row.

'I don't go to bed at all,' I apparently replied, 'I'm always here!'

Sydney Bridge

Girls' Life Brigade

I belonged to the 4th Leigh-on-Sea Company of the Girls' Life Brigade (GLB), as it was called at that time. The meetings were at West Leigh Baptist church. It is a Christian organisation that was based on the educational, spiritual and physical aspects of life. We did badge work and the badges were sewn onto our uniform sleeve. We also took the National Sunday School Union exams, so we built up a good Bible knowledge as well as doing a lot of craft work and other activities.

I stayed in GLB and later became a Warrant Officer before finally leaving at the age of twenty-two.

Lois Holmes

Priory Park

We were always fortunate with our parks in Southend. Priory Park was quite near my house when I was growing up and I could walk through it to get to school and to reach the various activities at St Mary's Church. The park has the remains of the old priory in the middle. Although the maze was small, it was quite exciting for a tiny child and there was also an attractive walled garden. We didn't appreciate that much as children!

LET US NOW PRAISE FAMOUS MEN
AND OUR FATHERS THAT BEGAT US

CERTIFICATE of MERIT

Awarded to
Keith Hall.

for Good Conduct *and* Regular Attendance

at St. Mary's (Prittlewell) Junior Sunday School

Signed N. B. Cable.

Keith Hall's Sunday School certificate.

There was also a muddy ditch that flowed into the Prittle Brook, and an old tree had fallen over the ditch so we could use it as a bridge on the way home. One day my friend was crossing when he slipped and fell. He came out completely plastered in mud.

Keith Hall

Dressed to impress

In 1937 I was three years old and I often went for walks with my father. We sometimes went down to the seafront – he used to tell me that we were taking a short cut, but it seemed a very long short cut. In those days I had quite definite ideas about what a young lady, even a very mini one, should wear. I always insisted on having a hat, gloves and a handbag!

Sometimes we went to Priory Park instead and as a special treat I had an ice cream, which cost one penny in old money.

Pamela Livingston (née Winn)

The dancing display

Once a year, in June, Miss Layborn put on a grand dancing display at the Palace Hotel, which was very impressive. Chandeliers hung from beautiful ceilings and there were mirrored walls. We thought we were in a castle when we went in. Miss Layborn came out in front of our parents in a flowing blue sequinned gown and wearing drop-diamond

15

earrings. The babies did their pieces first, followed by the older girls.

I made one very good friend called Jackie Busby. We both joined when we were five and continued until we were seventeen. As we grew older we helped Miss Layborn with the babies class. This meant leaving school ten minutes early, and the school agreed! Miss Layborn wanted me to teach dancing, but I went into the bank instead. Jackie and I still talk about Miss Layborn and how strict she was, but her teaching has helped us throughout our lives. Dancing was a very important part of my childhood.

Sally Hall

Sports day at Southend Stadium

During the Second World War, Southend Stadium was commandeered by the military and they decided to hold a sports day. I was about fourteen and I entered a one-hundred-yard handicap race. Because I was much smaller than everyone else I received a five-yard start and came in second or third. My prize was a fifteen-shilling war bond, a lot of money in those days. I also remember doing quite well in the long jump.

Frank Dudley

Beds on the floor

We moved to Southend from Hackney when I was six. As we lived in Meteor Road I went to Hamlet Court Road School. Later we moved to Seaforth Road, where my mother ran a boarding house. Sometimes, when we had a lot of people staying, my sister Kitty and I had to sleep on the floor, which was great fun.

Jean Lesser

The Palace Hotel still dominates Pier Hill.

Piles of cockle shells on the beach at Leigh.

Water Pits

It must have been around the time of the Great War. In those days builders were allowed to dig pits to hold water for their work, about 10ft by 10ft and 10ft deep. The mother of one boy always blew a horn to call him in for his meals. One day we heard the horn blown as usual and then more frequently and frantically. It transpired that the boy had fallen into a pit behind houses being built in Silversea Drive. No one was around to rescue him and he drowned. Later another boy fell into the same pit but this time several boys were there and we put a scaffold pole down the pit so the boy was able to climb to safety.

Arthur Hance

Cockles, shrimp and whitebait

My uncle owned the cockle sheds on Billet Wharf and my father owned ones further away. At first my father worked for his brothers, until he was able to branch out on his own. Then he and Uncle Alf had their own boat. When my grandfather on my mother's side died, he left two boats. One was a shrimper and the other was for whitebait, so my father then operated three boats. Usually he dealt with one firm in Billingsgate and sent the fish to London by train. However, on one occasion he sailed up with the whitebait ready for the Lord Mayor's Banquet. Another time he sailed to Greenwich because there was a dinner in the Painted Hall and whitebait was required. He unloaded his catch directly onto the jetty there.

As soon as we could walk we were taken out on one of the cockle boats. This was often when the boat was going to the Isle of Sheppey. We left at eight in the morning. Once we arrived we walked ashore and took a picnic with us.

I moved away from Leigh on my marriage in 1953 and finally returned in 1978.

Elvina Savill

Growing up by the sea

We lived in Victoria Avenue when I was a child – there were lots of big houses there then but they have all gone now.

My father used to take me to the seafront to feed the seagulls. When we went to the front I wanted to learn to swim, but I finally learnt in one of the open-air pools at Westcliff.

Babs Haywood

The beach artist

We lived in Kent when I was a child, but I came by train with my mother to visit my grandmother in Westcliff. We went to Gravesend and then over on the ferry. We travelled on steam trains with sepia pictures in the compartments, mostly scenes of Southend years ago, including some of the old bathing huts.

On my early visits we could go down to the beach, but once the war started there was barbed wire all the way along the seafront. Near Westcliff Station were some rather tatty flats, but they were taken over by soldiers and sailors. There was a lot of military activity in that area.

There was an artist close to the pier. I think that was just before the war. He had a large patch of sand and he dressed as Uncle Sam, standing on long stilts and drawing pictures in the sand with a stick. We threw money down to him.

The pier had a roller-skating rink and when my dad came too we sometimes went on the cars in Peter Pan's Playground and I sat on his lap. I also went on the paddle boats on the other side of the pier.

A favourite treat was to have a Rossi's ice cream. There was a shop called Goings at the top of Pier Hill that sold cockles and whelks.

Bill Sawford

Pamela Livingston with her granddaughter, Ashleigh, in 1989.

Tea at the palace

My mother had a friend, Ethel Lewis. She was a milliner and owned a shop in Hamlet Court Road. When she retired she moved away, but came back for a holiday when she stayed at the Palace Hotel. My sister and I were invited to tea one afternoon during her stay. The hotel foyer was very grand, with a sweeping staircase leading to the upper rooms. There were some huge Chinese pots standing near the entrance. We had to be on our very best behaviour in the restaurant and the waiters and waitresses seemed very intimidating.

Pamela Livingston

Days by the sea

In the holidays my mother packed a big lunch for the whole family and we walked the length of Bournemouth Park Road and over the

the seafood, especially the dishes of cockles. I have childhood memories of the Kursaal fairground and also of the pier, with its paddle steamers. The Golden Eagle and The Crested Eagle were also popular pleasure steamers.

Edward Clack

The fever hospital

My first school was Leigh North Street. In 1937 there was an outbreak of diphtheria. With a number of others I was taken into the fever hospital in Balmoral Road, Westcliff. There were wards for scarlet fever, measles, chicken pox, whooping cough and diphtheria. At visiting time the beds were turned round to face the windows. Parents were allowed to stand on stools so that they could talk through the windows, but they were not permitted to enter the wards.

While I was in the hospital I developed appendicitis, so I was whipped away to Rochford Hospital. The same ambulance that took me to Rochford then picked up my brother from home because I had given him diphtheria! The drivers were delighted because they only had to fumigate the ambulance once. While I was at Rochford they couldn't put me in with the children so I went in a ward with old ladies instead.

My mother had to see the almoner so that an assessment could be made to decide how much my family should contribute towards the cost of the operation. She was asked if she could afford five shillings and this was agreed. Strangely enough my brother also developed appendicitis while he was in the fever hospital. When mother went to see the almoner again it was decided that she should only be charged for one operation, so mother felt that she got us both done for the price of one! We were told later that a high fever can bring on appendicitis.

Elvina Savill

Edward Clack in 2003.

bridge to the seafront. We spent all day on the beach, close to the Brewery Road Bridge and the Kursaal, finally crawling home at around 5 p.m. By that time there were eight children in the family, so there was always someone to play with and we were never bored.

My family spent some time in India. Before this my father, Joseph Allen, who was in the Royal Artillery, lived in Rampart Street, Shoebury. He was a musician and a Staff Sergeant and he played first clarinet. On one occasion the conductor fell ill and my father took the baton when the band played at Southend Bandstand.

Audrey Dudley

Childhood visits to Southend

I've always loved Southend. As a child we used to come from London on day trips, often on Sunday school outings. We were very fond of

2 School

Westborough School

In 1915 I went to Westborough School in MacDonald Avenue, first as an infant when Miss Macintosh was the headmistress and then as a junior. Mr Hughes was the headmaster. The youngest children were in the building at the top of the road. Teachers were quite strict in those days, so you made sure you were always polite.

Bernard Riley

A strawberry tea!

After spending some time at Eastwood, I moved to Westborough School. That was when I was about eleven. I had to cross the Colemans Estate on foot to get there, or sometimes I was taken on a milk float. The big house was called Colemans Hall. It was owned by Mr Parish who kept cows in the fields. On one memorable occasion some of us went from Westborough for a strawberry tea at the house of Mr R.A. Jones, the well-known jeweller and benefactor to the town. I believe he did this for many of the school children in the town. He lived close to the bandstand at that time. While I was at Westborough School, Empire Day was always celebrated. This was a very important event and we all marched in the playground. In 1921 Lord and Lady Iveagh came and a Scottish girl did a sword dance.

From Westborough I went on the Southend Municipal Art School in Dowsett Avenue.

This was in a sort of tin hut. We all believed, rightly or wrongly, that the headmaster wore a wig, because some mornings it wasn't on straight! One of the teachers was Mr Jones and he was known as Bonzo. I studied wallpaper design, although I never used the skill. I left when I was fifteen.

Rhoda Deane

Hamlet Court Road School

Although we moved a number of times, I still went to Hamlet Court Road School – I loved it there. The headmistress was Miss Bird, who was very tiny but nice. I also liked Miss Hood, the history teacher, but I hated geography and I wasn't any good at running because I got tired. That was odd, because I could dance all night. When we were thirteen we were taken by bus to an evening school where I did cookery. I left school at fourteen.

Jean Lesser

Walking to school

My sister Rhoda and I both attended Eastwood School. It was a small country school with just Miss Morton's infants and two other classes, which were on either side of the hall. In the infants' class we had a stove with a fender. We walked along the single-track road that later become Prince Avenue – it took its name from Prince Henry, Duke of

Belfairs High School Festival, c. 1954. (Photograph by Shiner & Holmes)

Strawberry tea with Mr R.A. Jones, centre and Miss Bovey, the teacher, on his right, in 1921. Cecil Jones is on the right of the back row.

21

Gloucester, who opened it in 1926. We went out to wave flags when he came down.

In 1925 I moved to Chalkwell School. I walked backwards and forwards four times a day, because I always came home for lunch at midday. The classes at Chalkwell were much larger than the ones at Eastwood, with forty-eight to fifty-two in each class.

Frank Bagnald

Changing schools

I moved from St Michael's Anglican School to West Leigh in 1944 and I really noticed the difference at meal times. At St Michael's we always had tablecloths and all the food was well presented. At West Leigh I don't think the cooking was done on the premises. We ate in the school hall and there were huge containers of mashed potato. Then there was tapioca with a dollop of jam. There were certainly no tablecloths!

Lois Holmes

Changes in education

I started off at Chalkwell School at the age of five. Then, when I was nine, I went to Westborough School briefly before moving to Hamlet Court Road School for two years. This was the time when the whole system changed. After that there were separate junior and senior schools, whereas when I started you usually went to the same school from five to fourteen. I spent the next four years at Southend High, the grammar school. At that time it was at Victoria Circus. In 1937 a new building was completed in Prittlewell Chase, which was great for me as I lived only a few minutes' walk away. I stayed for four years rather than the usual five at grammar school, but I didn't really leave the school – the school left me! In 1940 nearly all the pupils were evacuated to the Midlands and I was one of the few to be left behind.

Frank Dudley

West Leigh School in 1944 with criss-cross window protection.

Belfairs School Festival c. 1954. Sally Hall is fourth from the left in the front row.

Schooldays were fun!

I went first to St Andrew's School, a little independent one. It was rather like going into your own house. The headmistress was Mrs Carney and I still see one of the teachers.

From St Andrews I moved to Fairfax High, which was mixed then. In 1953 it was turned into a boys' school, so then I moved to Belfairs High for Girls. I loved it there because it was new and we had lots of sport, cookery and needlework – all the things I liked best. I represented the school for long jump and ran in the relay. We never had homework and for me school was fun. I have just been to the fiftieth anniversary and met up with some of my old school friends.

Sally Hall

Gas masks

I was five years old when I went to Greenaways School in Lifstan Way, and it was wartime. My very first lesson was painting; I had four colours to use and just dubbed them in. My gas mask was green and Dad had a black one. We kept them under the stairs with Dad's Home Guard gun.

Next I went to Southchurch Hall School. I loved both schools and, because I was sporty, I could get away with anything.

John Horsley

No holidays

My parents never went away on holiday. They always said that, as we lived in a seaside town, there was no reason for us to go away to another one. Also, my father worked a twelve-hour day throughout the year. However, while my brother and I were in hospital my parents nipped off on holiday. Such a thing had never happened before.

Elvina Savill

Westcliff High School in Victoria Avenue

At eleven I passed the scholarship and went to the Commercial Secondary School in Victoria Avenue. Within a year it was renamed Westcliff High School and it educated both boys and girls. At that time, if you didn't get a scholarship, you had to pay for secondary education. I think it was about two guineas a term. The school was in a very large house called Belsfield. It was opened because the town was growing and it was felt necessary to have a new secondary school. Southend High School for Boys was at Victoria Circus in the building that had been Southend Technical Institute and later became Southend Municipal College. Eventually the boys of Westcliff High School moved to a new building in Eastwood Boulevard. The girls remained in Victoria Avenue until their new school was built next door to the boys.

Discipline was quite strict in those days. I was talking in a lesson on one occasion and was told to stand outside the door. Unfortunately, the headmaster came along and ordered me into his study where I got the cane! I did move into the new building, but only for one term as I left after taking my matriculation.

Bernard Riley

Abdication

I was still at Leigh North Street School when King Edward VIII abdicated. We were called into the school hall where we listened to the abdication speech.

Later, I was evacuated with the school. My mother didn't want me to go and I was only away for a year before I returned. The whole town was evacuated with only around 500 families left, but fortunately there was still one of every type of shop. Because so many children and teachers had left the town, schools were unable to function properly so for a while my schooling was badly disrupted.

Elvina Savill

Ten Green Bottles and fluffy balls

I went to St Mary's School, Prittlewell, during the war. My first classroom was in the middle

The Osborne name is still well known in Leigh.

Above: *Keith Hall's first classroom at St Mary's School.*

Below: *Eastwood High School in 1952. Clockwise from the back are Jean Austen, Doreen Laxton, Rita Jefferson, Wendy Jeffrey and Lois Hance.*

of the building and it protruded into the play-ground. We sat in little chairs with curved backs. When there were air raids we had to go out to underground shelters in the play-ground, and I remember singing Ten Green Bottles and other songs as planes flew over-head. Sometimes we made fluffy balls by winding wool round and round cardboard milk bottle tops; French knitting using a wooden cotton reel was also popular. The shelters always smelt musty, presumably because they were damp.

Keith Hall

Secondary school

After sitting the scholarship exam I went to Eastwood High School. On the first day I was terrified. I'd always been a very quiet, docile child and the headmaster swept into the first assembly wearing his gown. We sat on the floor, leaving a gangway down the middle. At the end of that assembly he told us all that one of the older boys had been killed during the holiday when climbing a pylon. One of my classmates had to be taken out – he had been her brother.

At the Easter of our first year Mr Cooper became headmaster and he was very different. The first headmaster I feared, but the second I respected. That was the way I felt about my parents: I respected them so I wanted to do well for them.

Lois Holmes

The final year at St Mary's

My teacher in my last year at St Mary's School came from Cornwall and sang in the church choir. Mr Richardson was the headteacher and I also remember Miss Cable and Miss Harvey.

One part of the school was much older than the rest – it had a second floor and that was where the headmaster's office was located. If you were called up there it could be good, but it might equally be bad and could mean the cane if you had done something wrong.

The toilets were outside and open to the sky. Being a church school, every Wednesday morning we went to a service in the church and we walked through the churchyard to get there. Canon Gowing took most of those services. When I left St Mary's I went to Westcliff High School for Boys.

Keith Hall

The school pantomime

I went to Eastwood Infant and Junior Schools. We lived in a bungalow in Snakes Lane, almost opposite the school gate.

Eastwood Junior School's Class 2 with Mr Browning in around 1970.

Eastwood Junior School Pantomime, c. 1970.

There was a swimming pool in the grounds, but the water was always very cold because it wasn't sunk in the ground, but rested on the surface.

Mr Browning was my favourite teacher. He had a beard and greying hair and he was extremely talented. Every year he wrote the school pantomime, including all the songs, and put everything to music, played the piano and produced the whole thing. I was a South Sea dancer in one of his productions in 1970. I wore a yellow sarong and brown body paint.

One thing I remember, which I suppose is pretty horrific now, is that we had a spelling and a tables test every week and anyone who didn't do well in these tests got the slipper from the headmaster – definitely not what would be expected now!

Mary Wigley (née Clamp)

Matric during evacuation

As a boy I went to Bournemouth Park School and then to Southend High. The grammar school was at Victoria Circus until it moved to a new building and then, in 1940, we were evacuated to Mansfield where we took our matriculation. That was at the Queen Elizabeth Grammar School, although we could only go for half of each day because we had to share the school. We came home after six months. After we returned there were often mobile ack-ack guns in Branksome Road where I lived.

When we walked home after dark there was sometimes flack falling all around. Once the school had moved to its new building there were air-raid shelters in the playing field. We had to go down steps or walk on a plank to get into the shelter and one day I fell off the plank into several inches of water, because underground shelters were always very damp.

German bombers used the pier as a finger pointing towards Southend Aerodrome. The school was on the way and it had a flat roof, which they probably thought was part of the aerodrome, so they dropped their bombs. The library went and so did the assembly hall, complete with the organ that had been moved from Victoria Circus. The library had beautiful oak panelling.

Dennis Haywood

Miss Rose

When we went into our second year at Eastwood High School a new deputy head-teacher arrived, Miss Rose, and she became our form teacher. We all lined up outside our form room on her first morning.
'Be quiet,' she said. We weren't. 'BE QUIET!', she bellowed, and we were. I thought she was about a hundred at the time, but now I realise she was probably only in her forties.

Miss Rose was a wonderful teacher who taught us a love of history and RE that I have never lost – those lessons really came alive. She was very strict, but also very fair, and she was also in charge of the school library. To find out which books we liked we were asked to do a summary. We always got house points for doing that and it really made us want to read. She stayed as our form teacher until we left and had a tremendous influence on us all.

Lois Holmes

A wartime schoolboy

School dinners and the siren go together in my mind. When I was a child, if we were in the middle of lunch when the siren went, we picked up our plates and made for the shelter in the middle of the playground. We thought that was great fun. Part of the time I was at Brewery Road School and later at

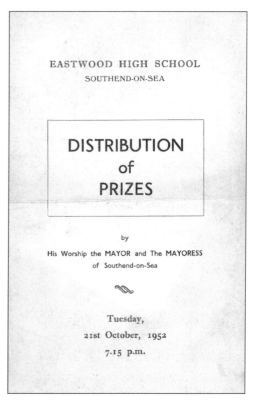

EASTWOOD HIGH SCHOOL
SOUTHEND-ON-SEA

DISTRIBUTION
of
PRIZES

by

His Worship the MAYOR and The MAYORESS
of Southend-on-Sea

Tuesday,
21st October, 1952
7.15 p.m.

1952 Eastwood High School Prizegiving. Lois Hance won the History Prize.

Southchurch Hall School, where we had a fire station in the playground. There were a couple of fire engines kept there.

Occasionally we saw dogfights over the Thames Estuary. One plane came down on the London Hotel on the corner of Tylers Avenue. I saw that happen. If there were raids when we were at home we usually hid under the kitchen table, rather than in the garden Anderson shelter. That was covered in turf and was extremely damp. My mother kept chickens in the back garden and I can remember making their mash out of potato peelings. Those chickens gave us a good supply of meat and eggs. Not that we killed them ourselves – my grandfather came down from London to do that, although we did help to pluck them. At that time we were living in a rented house

Ray Box in 2003.

off York Road. It didn't have a proper bath so we used a galvanised one instead. Saturday night was the time for baths and the oven was lit and the door opened as we had our baths in the kitchen. Afterwards the water was emptied out of the back door and it flowed down the garden.

Ray Box

The new boy

Going to Westcliff High School was quite an event because I had to have a school uniform for the first time. This was bought at Perhams' in the London Road at Westcliff. I needed a blazer, tie, shirt and rugby boots. The headmaster was Mr Henry Cloke, a large, impressive character. He wore a gown and was quite a disciplinarian.

On my first day I had to sit in the gymnasium with all the other new entrants. Our names were gradually called out, starting with 2A – for some reason all the first year classes started with '2'. Boys went out until almost everyone else had gone, but I was still sitting there. I began to wonder if I was on the list! I started off in 2D, but fortunately things got better and after the first term I went up to 2B. At that point I started doing Spanish and Latin. Latin was taught by Mr Cloke, which was rather frightening as I had already missed one term.

There was an initiation ceremony for new boys. At the top of the school playing field there was a sloping bank, which proba-

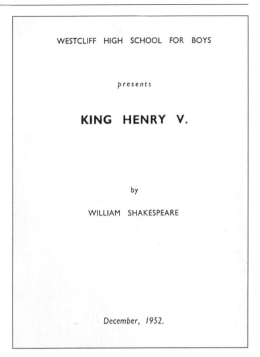

WESTCLIFF HIGH SCHOOL FOR BOYS

presents

KING HENRY V.

by

WILLIAM SHAKESPEARE

December, 1952.

The 1952 programme for King Henry V. Keith Hall played 'An English Lord'.

The Municipal College Art School blazer badge c. 1924.

bly only went down for ten or twelve feet, but newcomers were dragged down backwards by seniors and then deposited at the bottom.

Keith Hall

Watery stew!

My father was in the Army and my first four years were spent in India. On our return we moved into a council house in Bournemouth Park Road. I started at Bournemouth Park Road School in 1927 where I was made milk monitor. Every child had one third of a pint of milk each day. Before giving out the bottles I made sure that I found the one with the most cream on top, and this I carefully hid in the corner for myself! I was very keen on sport and I raced for the school at the annual Inter-Schools Sports Day, held at the Jones Memorial Ground. I was the champion girl runner of my school.

From Bournemouth Park I went to Wentworth School, which was fun. At that time there were fields all round the school. I thoroughly enjoyed my time there, but one of my favourite lessons was cookery. I always came last when the stews were tasted because I took a spoonful out from time to time to taste and then made up the quantity with water!

After passing a test I moved on to the Art Department of the Municipal College.

Audrey Dudley

Young scientist!

Sidney Cooper was the headmaster of Westborough when I first taught there, but later Miss Wilshire was appointed. At that

Sydney Bridge in 2003.

time the school was still mixed, although later it became a girls' school. One day a large boy prefect dragged a small lad into the head-mistress' room saying, 'He tried to blow up the lavatories.' These were outside, and apparently the boy had a firework and had decided to see what would happen if he dropped it down the pan. He found out – it shattered into a thousand pieces!

Anne Elliott

Secretarial training

Fifteen was the school leaving age in 1952. I then took an exam and went to the Southend Municipal College at Victoria Circus to follow an 'O' Level course in commercial subjects. I learnt shorthand and typing and soon discovered that I especially liked accounts. Our teacher was an accountant. After we did our first mock exam he held up my paper and said he had tried very hard to find a mistake on the paper but he couldn't. The only snag was I had only answered the first question and I should have completed five! After that I learnt to forget about perfect presentation on my papers and become much quicker.

After passing the exams I took my first job in London and I used to travel up each day on the steam train from Leigh.

Lois Holmes

Unmade roads

Having passed the scholarship exam I went to Westcliff High School, where I was put in the 'A' Stream. It was a new building then, opened at Easter 1926. I went there in September. I finally passed my matriculation examination with honours in French, German

31

and maths. My only real disappointment there was that the school played rugby, not football!

To get to school I often cycled down Shakespeare Drive because Brook Road, now Priory Crescent, was impassable in winter and Fairfax Drive was unmade until you reached Shakespeare Drive. It was only in later years that you could cycle right the way through. I left school in 1930.

Sydney Bridge

A sudden departure

My first school was St Audrey's in Thorpe Bay, but the school building has now been converted into flats. We wore orange blazers that had a very special smell and our badge was embroidered in gold thread. The start of the war caused some disruption to my schooling – at one point we moved to Leigh and I went to West Leigh School. That was a memorable move. The headmaster, a large man, came into the classroom and pinched my cheeks.

'What's your name little girl?' he boomed. I slammed down the desk lid, grabbed my coat and stormed out of the school, never to return!

Diana Ayre

Westcliff High School for Girls

After passing the scholarship I went to Westcliff High School. It was very large, completely different from my primary school. It was apparently the first school in England to have parquet flooring. Miss Wilkinson was the headmistress and she was strict, but very fair. This was 1945 and it was still difficult to get hold of new clothes, and although I needed school uniform, money was short. My grandmother was good at needlework and knitting so she made many of the things I needed. Even so, a prefect told me off one day in front of my friends because I wasn't wearing the correct school dress!

Pamela Livingston

3 By the Sea

Excursion trains

I was born in 1931 and was around eight when we started going to Southend from Becontree on the Fenchurch Street line. There were special excursion trains, because not all trains stopped at our station. We arrived in Southend at the station halfway down the High Street.

There were two trains, one leaving at about 8.30 a.m. and the second an hour later. Not everyone had holidays in those days so trips to the nearest seaside town were very important. We took sandwiches and drinks and we would spend the day there. We went on the pier where there were boat trips. After 1945, we looked out for anything left behind from the war, including the remains of a section of the Mulberry Harbour. There wasn't much sand, but we paddled and went out on the mud when the tide was out.

The clothes worn at the seaside were very different from those worn today. They were much heavier and many of the men still wore suits. When we paddled, the girls tucked their skirts in their knickers and older women held their skirts up out of the water.

Going home was the worst part of the whole day. You had to be at the station at the right time for your train and it was always jam-packed. The ticket collector only let a certain number through the barrier at a time to avoid overcrowding on the platform.

Iris Campbell

Beside the sea

My childhood playground was the seafront, between the pier and the Kursaal. Of course there was barbed wire, but there were places where you could get through and swim. The fishermen still came in with their catches and you could buy fresh fish from the jetty. Later, my father became a licensed victualler and he used to buy a box of fish for his customers and the family.

My other main play area was Southchurch Park. Cricket and football were my favourite games, although much of my time was taken up with church activities, including Scouts and choir practices and also the youth club. At one time I went to ballroom-dancing classes.

Ray Box

A grand day out!

We loved the Kursaal. To get inside we passed through two rotating barrels. I have special memories of the Laughing Policeman in the entrance hall and the Caterpillar ride. The Cyclone was amazing. It was the biggest ride ever at that time. It was a giant scenic railway and you had to be really brave to go on that. The Wall of Death was memorable too, with Tornado Smith racing round and the whole arena shaking. There was the Water Shoot too, and the Dive Bomb. That had a long arm and a bomb shape on each end. You had to be strapped in because it turned over. It is

Iris Campbell in 2003.

stilts. There were removable shutters round the front and we used a curtain and changed behind that. Bench seats lined the front half and we had a boat hanging on the back with a mast and sails, but it could also be used as a rowing boat. When the tide was in we could swim from the hut steps, as the tide went up to the back wall.

Mary Wigley (née Clamp)

Living by the sea

As a child I don't remember going often to the seaside, but when I was a young man I would take my young lady for a walk along the front, and especially beside the band-stand. In the evening there were fairy lights all around the bandstand and it was a very popular place to walk and listen to the band. Prittlewell Square was popular too, with its attractive fountains.

Bernard Riley

Leigh Swimming Pool

My first memory of Southend seafront is of barbed wire. It stretched as far as I could see. On one occasion I was in Leigh with an older boy and his friends. He was meant to be looking after me but they all ran down the road to the Leigh Cliffs and on to Leigh Swimming Pool. At that time it was shut up and it was impossible to reach the pool because of the barbed wire. However, the boys managed to get in, which I knew was extremely naughty, so I ran back to tell someone what was happening! Later on I took my Girls' Brigade swimming badge in the Leigh pool.

When one of my brothers was born I stayed with a family in Leigh. Their older son collected me from school and took me to St Clement's Hall, which was very crowded. It

nothing compared with the sort of thing you see now, but we thought it was fantastic. Then there was wrestling in the Coronation Dome. That was purpose built and it stood where the new houses are now. Once they were built, wrestling moved into the ballroom before going to the Cliffs Pavilion.

We also went along the pier sometimes, on what was called the Bubble Train.

Southend was an exciting place. As a child a visit to the town was a highlight of the summer. When I first came to live in the town I was sad at leaving my family, but now there is nowhere else I would rather live.

Doreen Sawford

Beach huts at Thorpe Bay

My grandparents owned a beach hut at Thorpe Bay and we went there every sunny day during the school holidays and at week-ends. It seemed very tall to me as it stood on

Left: *Mary Clamp with her cousin Jane on the steps of the family beach hut in 1966.*

Right: *Thorpe Bay Broadway, where many properties had 999-year leases.*

was being used as a civic restaurant where you could have a full meal for one shilling. There was a strong smell of food, quite different from cooking smells at home.

Lois Holmes

999-year leases!

In the school holidays and at weekends in the summer I went with my parents to the beach at Thorpe Bay. This was while I was still at primary school. We took the bus from Sutton Road Cemetery to the Central Station in Southend and then caught a train to Thorpe Bay. After that we walked through the Broadway to spend the day on the beach. This was in the 1920s and the Broadway was still being built. It was the first time I had ever seen 999-year leases advertised!

Sydney Bridge

A special ice cream

The war was over, but only just. On a very hot day I went with Brian, who lived opposite, to the Westcliff Swimming Pool. As he was six months older than I was he was supposed to look after me. We set off on the number 17 bus, which stopped outside what is now the Beecroft Art Gallery, and then walked over the cliffs and down to the pool. Brian had the money.

Inside, we swam together, but split up to get changed. We arranged to meet outside once we were ready. I went out and waited and waited, but he didn't come. Later he said he had waited and I didn't come. It was quite busy so that's possibly how we missed each other. Of course I hadn't any money and the only way to get back home was to walk right along the seafront until I reached Leigh. Then I could walk straight up the hill and I would eventually reach my house.

Rossi has been a popular supplier of ice cream to thousands of Southend visitors.

It was extremely hot, and when I reached Chalkwell I saw a family and they had just bought ice creams. That was still quite a novelty. One little girl was crying that she didn't want hers, and I gazed at it longingly. Her father said, 'If you don't behave you won't have it. Are you going to eat it or not?'

'No!' she yelled.

'Very well, then I shall give it to this little girl,' he said, and he did. I made sure she didn't get a second chance and I must admit it was the loveliest ice cream I have ever tasted.

When I finally arrived home Brian was already there, because he had been able to catch the bus!

Lois Holmes

Trips to the seaside

Erith in Kent was my home town, but sometimes my grandfather would bring me to Southend for the day on a Sunday. At that time it was very much a 'Kiss me Quick' sort of place. I loved it. I always had a stick of rock and we would go to the Kursaal, where I really enjoyed the slot machines. As I got older I came down on the outings from the Working Men's Club of Kent, travelling on the 'beano' coach with my aunts. There were crates of beer in the back of the coach so that they could stop by the roadside. We always stopped at The Albion on the A13 on the way and then at The Ivy House along the seafront.

Many beach huts at Thorpe Bay are on stilts.

In the evening we loved the lights. This was the outing for the ladies – the men had their own outing.

Doreen Sawford

Beach huts for summer days

As a child we lived in Thorpe Bay and the house came complete with a beach hut which stood on stilts. We also had a key to use the gardens around Thorpe Bay Tennis Club. Later, when my children were small, we hired a beach hut at Shoebury for the whole of the month of August. Other families joined us and we began to spread out, so we hired a second hut next door.

Diana Ayre

Trippers to Southend

Between the wars, trips ran from London to Southend for half a crown, including admission to the Kursaal. That area got extremely crowded, so most residents kept away. Because we always went to Thorpe Bay we got to know the regular visitors and the owners of the beach huts.

Sydney Bridge

Cycling to Southend

When I was seventeen I started cycling to Southend. In fact, the first long cycle ride that I ever did was from Becontree to Southend. Later, when I joined a proper cycling club, I was asked if I'd done much cycling and where

Iris Campbell and her fellow cyclists on the Southend road in 1950.

I'd been. It was only later that I discovered that almost everybody proudly claimed to have ridden all the way to Southend! These rides always involved going up Bread and Cheese Hill, which was really hard work, especially on the old, heavy bikes that were used in those days.

Iris Campbell

Living in a 'safe house'

We came to Southend in the early 1940s. After being bombed out a couple of times, my mother wanted to move away from London. At that time my father was in the Merchant Navy, on the Russian convoys, so we only saw him every couple of years. He was torpedoed three times and was finally invalided out of the Merchant Navy. He weighed about nineteen stone and had a big black beard. In my earliest memories of him he always seemed to be wearing sea boots. At first he didn't have a set-

tled job, so he worked with the lifeboat crew and he also became a lifesaver on the pier, which meant that if anyone fell in the water from the pier he would jump in and rescue them.

At that time our home became a 'safe house' for the lifeboat. We lived in St Leonard's Road then, just off York Road, so we were close to the seafront. Anyone who was rescued could come to us for a bed for the night and we always kept dry clothes ready for these sudden visitors. It did mean that we were sometimes turned out of our beds for the night! Since then we have always supported the RNLI.

Ray Box

The Hoover lady!

Every year I took part in the carnival parade – the money went to Southend Hospital in those days. One year I had to stand on top of

Although damaged in many accidents, the pier is still an impressive sight.

the float dressed in a red suit and holding up a Hoover. I was scared stiff of heights so I kept telling myself not to look down! It took three hours for the procession to pass, and the people watching weren't allowed to sit on the kerb, but they had to have deckchairs. I first took part when I was fourteen.

Jean Lesser

Peter Pan's Playground

My sister loved Peter Pan's Playground. One day she disappeared from home and mum called the police, but dad finally found her at Peter Pan's.

A nurse had a little hut in one corner and there were swings, some of which were very old fashioned and painted in different colours. There was also the 'Crooked House' and bumper cars. The railway had round carriages painted with bright stripes of red, yellow and green, and they turned round as you rode in them.

On the other side of the pier was a boating pool, but it wasn't very deep and there was a lot of muck in it. Next door was a replica of the *Golden Hind* with waxworks inside. We thought it was marvellous.

John Horsley

The whitebait festival

There is still a whitebait festival in Southend but the venue isn't fixed. It has been held at the end of the pier, on one of the yacht club boats and at the Cliffs Pavilion. This is an important event because whitebait, although small, is very much a local fish.

Geoffrey Ayre

The Scenic Railway

One of the most popular rides at the Kursaal was the Scenic Railway, which was huge. As a family we didn't usually go to the Kursaal, but some cousins came and took me with them and the only ride I can remember going on was the Scenic Railway. When I finally staggered away I decided that was the first and last time. I could never work out what fun people had leaving their stomachs behind as they hurtled round in tiny cars.

Lois Holmes

Visits to the seaside

I first went to Southend in 1937, just before the war. We travelled down on the LNER line from East Ham. We always went straight to the beach where we played with our buckets and spades while the adults sat on deckchairs. This was always close to the pier. When the tide went out we walked for what seemed to be miles on the mud. Close to the shore, soft mud oozed between our toes.

Occasionally we walked both ways on the pier instead of taking the train. At lunchtime we loved to have fish and chips, and in the afternoon a man came along the beach with a big tray of pineapple slices. I saw jellied eels for sale, but I never tried them.

Sometimes we went to Leigh. We would get off the train at Chalkwell and then walk to Leigh, the main reason for which was to see the cockle sheds. There were mounds of seashells and sometimes during the day there would be a delicious plate of cockles.

Victor Salmon

Trips to Southend

When I was nursing at Rochford, by the end of the month we were often left with only sixpence. We usually chose to go to Southend, and if we went by bus it was a three-penny return. Usually we walked — it cost three pence to get into the Hippodrome. Our time off was very limited — just two hours each day at first, but we had one evening free occasionally.

On Sundays we went to church. This might be at Prittlewell, but on Sunday mornings we usually went to Rochford church because we were allowed to go there in uniform. We couldn't come into the town in uniform. In the village we had to use the back lane to return to Acacia House. We walked to Prittlewell church through Manners Way and Priory Park, before going up the hill. We walked a great deal, often going through Cherry Orchard Lane or to Ashingdon. Stambridge Mills was another popular place to visit. I didn't swim when we got there, but many of the nurses did.

Betty Riley

The Never Never Land

Sometimes we went to the Never Never Land on the cliffs. We walked down the paths in the evening when all the lights were on and there were all sorts of little grottos and illuminated working models.

I also remember going down the pier and trying not to step on the cracks. We used to walk one way and then come back on the

Geoffrey and Diana Ayre in their garden in 2003.

Victor Salmon, seen here in 2003, is now a keen artist.

The Never Never Land continues to take children into a world of fantasy.

train. That was the most memorable part of any visit to Southend.

David Wigley

Southend parks

When we first arrived in Eastwood we were on a new estate and no one had much idea about gardening. We all worked very hard, but we had to go to the parks to let the children run around. We especially liked Belfairs Wood. I still go there, but now I take my grandchildren. The equipment for children in the parks is fantastic now.

When we moved in our neighbour was Ken McCreadie. He was the Chief Parks Officer so he was in charge of all the parks and recreation grounds. At that time Southend had a national collection of pelargoniums and these were exhibited at the Chelsea Flower Show where he and his team won gold medals in the 1960s and 1970s. His advice was invaluable when we were young gardeners.

Maureen Ollett

A very wet carnival!

On one of our visits to the town it was carnival time. It used to be wonderful. Starting in Leigh, it moved into Chalkwell Avenue and then along the seafront to the pier, finally reaching the Kursaal and Southchurch Park East. However, on that first occasion there was torrential rain and we were allowed to shelter in Leigh Library by climbing through a back window.

Later, as mayor, I was involved in judging the dog show and also the Beautiful Baby contest during carnival week – two of the most difficult tasks faced during my year of office!

Geoffrey Ayre

From the pier to the Kursaal

A visit to the Kursaal was great fun. It was most spectacular because we'd never seen anything like that before. We were used to ordinary fair grounds where everything was packed away after the weekend, but being on a permanent site, the rides at the Kursaal were large and impressive. I well remember getting soaked on the Water Shoot.

A walk along the seafront between the pier and the Kursaal was noisy and exciting. There were slot machines, ice cream and candy floss sellers. Rossi's ice cream was unusually soft and very popular. Then there were fish and chip shops and many pubs, often filled with people who had come on coach trips and works outings. When the tide went out there was an enormous stretch of mud, but the mud was supposed to be good for you.

If you went on the pier there were always lots of fishermen and you had to walk around the fishing lines. When I first went there the trains to the end were open and rattled loudly. Because the pier is over a mile long you felt as if you were far out to sea when you reached the end. Quite often we didn't ride, but walked instead, and at the very end of the pier there were more slot machines.

Iris Campbell

Lacking buoyancy!

My grandma had a beach hut at the bottom of Thorpe Hall Avenue and we went there a lot with the family. I love the seaside and will abandon housework at a moment's notice to go down to the beach. Although I've always enjoyed being by the sea, for many years I couldn't swim. My mother tried to teach me and I've had swimming lessons all over the place, but without great success. In the end I was told I'm not very buoyant! Even so, I love going in the water and I can swim now, but I

The Kursaal is now greatly reduced in size, but the dome remains an impressive landmark.

never go out of my depth. I still almost live on the beach in summer and enjoy our own hut now.

Sally Hall

Steamboats from the pier

As a teenager I used to go with my parents on the steamboats which ran from the end of the pier. Four or five came in each day. One ran to Margate, another to Sheerness, Chatham and Rochester and yet another to Herne Bay. There were separate queues for each of the dif-ferent destinations. When the boats came alongside we all surged forward. The return fare to Sheerness was 1s 6d and the return fare to Chatham and Rochester cost 2s. That was a very interesting trip because Sheerness had a pier in those days and that was the first stop. Then we went on to Chatham, which was still a flourishing naval establishment at that time. You could see warships moored there. After that we went on to Rochester where we had two hours ashore to visit the cathedral or the castle before the return trip.

There were also the Belle Steamers. These went round to Clacton and Yarmouth.

43

Sally Hall and her family leave a pier steamer in around 1949.

On one occasion, after we were married, my wife and I went by boat to Margate for our holiday. One of the boats that went to Rochester was the *Medway Queen*. She was involved in the Dunkirk rescue and got rather knocked about. After the war, once people started going abroad for their holidays, steamboats became less popular and they gradually finished. The *Medway Queen* is now laid up in a creek along the River Medway, but there are plans to restore and refloat her.

Bernard Riley

Walks along the prom

We moved to Cranleigh Drive, Leigh-on-Sea on my fifteenth birthday. The first Easter after our arrival, on the Good Friday, I walked with my mother and father along the seafront to Southend and then back again. That was a very long walk, so we didn't get further than the pier.

Sometimes we walked beside the cockle sheds in Leigh where they sold shellfish. I did try the cockles, but I didn't like them much! There was always a very distinctive smell of salt and ozone at Leigh. Shells were piled high by the sheds and there was a lovely crunchy sound as you walked on them.

Further along towards Hadleigh, houseboats were moored and you could see them from the train as you came towards the town. Some were quite ramshackle, but others were rather lovely. They went right along the coast to the Benfleet area.

Pamela Bissell

Lois Hance and her family enjoy the Southend illuminations in around 1950.

The illuminations

After the war, Southend became a wonderland at night when the annual illuminations were switched on. We went as a family group to see them, and we also enjoyed the carnival. The big Saturday procession started in Leigh and went along to the Kursaal. One year I followed the procession. I was still quite young, so it was probably the first carnival after the war.

As I went along I was amazed to see people throwing money into nets. Then I saw a penny on the ground, so I picked it up. It didn't occur to me that I should have put it in a net. Further along I found other coins and ended up with twelve pence – a fortune to me. I reached the Golden Mile and there were arcades with fruit machines and I realised that if you put your money in you were likely to get even more back, so I tried. My twelve pennies soon disappeared and I didn't get any money back! That day I learnt that gambling was a mug's game. When I got home my parents explained that this was a form of stealing because the money was meant for charity, so that day I learnt two very useful lessons that I've never forgotten.

Lois Holmes

4 By the Church

Two popular churches

St Mary's church, Prittlewell, had two even-songs before the war and Mr Penny, the organist, played for them both. The first service finished at 6.30 p.m. Then both the West and the Vestry doors were opened so that the congregation could go out. In the meantime a crowd gathered outside the South door, on the East Street side. Then people swarmed in to fill the pews and another service began at 7.00 p.m.

There were probably two reasons why the church was so popular in those days. It was certainly more important in most people's lives, but also Canon Gowing was a great draw. He would have special services for people like yachtsmen on a Sunday afternoon. Notices were put up that said things like: 'Yachtsmen Ahoy! See you at Prittlewell Church on Sunday.'

There were various themed services on Sunday afternoons, including a footballers' service. They really pulled the people in.

Another well-loved vicar, the Revd J.J. Whitehouse, was at St John's, Southend. Many of the owners of the big shops in the High Street went there and some of them became church wardens.

The war really changed things for the church. Afterwards, many people didn't return, for a variety of reasons. At St Mary's the second evensong soon stopped.

Bernard Riley

The four Miss Fowlers

As children we went to Sunday school at St Lawrence church, Eastwood. The four Miss Fowlers, who lived at Cockethurst Farmhouse, took all the classes. May and Rainee were twins and the eldest. Then there was Ethel and Gladys, the youngest. All four dressed alike and all the dresses were made by Rainee.

Inside the house there was a large kitchen, a living room, then a hall and finally you reached another room with a huge table. This was where two girls sat on either side and the parents sat one at each end. On Sunday no work was done.

The sisters were wonderful to us when we were children. At Christmas time they always gave a marvellous party for the children of the area at the barn in the old Vicarage grounds. Every other year we were given a text to hang on the wall. They made things like nightdress cases so that every child had a present. Later they gave the Mayflower Window to the church. Now the whole family is buried at Eastwood church.

Rhoda Deane

The church at war

I used to go fire watching with the vicar before I was called up. You had to watch out for incendiary bombs, which didn't do too much damage themselves, but they set fire to

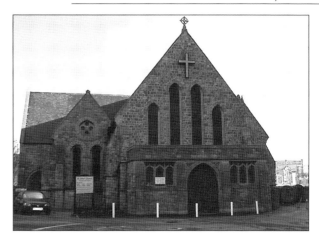

St John's church stands behind the Palace Hotel close to the High Street.

everything close by. One night each week I stayed at the church and another night I would be at the Rates Office in the town where three of us were on duty every night. Luckily nothing ever happened.

At the church I would sleep in the vestry until the siren sounded. Then I got up, put on my tin hat and was ready to go up on the roof if necessary. Buckets of water and sand were kept up there ready to pour over any bombs. Although the roof sloped you could walk around the side, which was flat. We had a proper rota at the church for fire watching, and if the siren went during a service Mr Penny, the organist, who was also the chief warden, would pick up his tin hat and gas mask and leave.

Many churches had to give up evening services during the war, but not St Mary's. Our vicar organised the making of enormous blinds, like huge sails. They were made of shiny black material. The sidesmen hoisted them up before the service started and every window was covered. To protect the porch there was a zigzag screen, so no light escaped. After the service the blinds were rolled up and left on the pews ready for the next week. I believe there are still a couple of pulleys left where they used to pull up the blinds.

Bernard Riley

Marriage in 1947 – the year of the big freeze

A fortnight after my demob, in the January of 1947, my wife and I were married at St Mary's church, Prittlewell. It was the worst winter in living memory. After the service the choirboys threw snowballs instead of confetti! Snow started the week after I left the forces and it didn't end until Easter. After our marriage we moved into a flat nearby in Priory Avenue, but later we were given a flat in South Avenue belonging to Southend United Football Club in Sutton Road and close to the ground.

Frank Dudley

Wesley Hall

Pastor Belcher was the minister of Wesley Hall Methodist chapel in West Road. Because it was closer to our house than St Mary's, we went there to Sunday school. Pastor Belcher had been in the First World War and he wore his old uniform throughout the Second World War as well. He and his wife loved the children and used to put on silent film shows for us, which we thought were great. Sometimes a conjuror came to entertain, dressed in Chinese costume and doing amazing tricks.

At Christmas there was always a party with a present for every child. These were sent by a church in Canada.

One of the highlights of the year was the Sunday school anniversary service. We sat in the choir seats at the front of the church and sang and recited poems. In front of our seats was a rail with holes just large enough to take tiny individual Holy Communion glasses. They were also just the right size to take an old penny. Often our collection ended up firmly stuck in those holes.

Pamela Livingston

St Erkenwald's

I belonged to St Erkenwald's church during the war. I was a choirboy and later became head choirboy with Len Thorby, who became a local builder. Len's mother donated the East window of Holy Trinity church. My father was the group Scoutmaster at St Erkenwald's. He was also a bell ringer and, at one point, the verger. I became a server.

I continued at the church until the priest in charge announced that unless he had a hundred per cent turnout from the all the youth movements of the church then he would close them down. Sadly, this happened. Previously there had been a thriving choir, youth club, Guide, Brownie and Cub groups. The choir moved more or less en masse to St John's, but I didn't stay there for long because I went into the Army.

Ray Box

A charismatic minister

My family moved to Leigh in 1947. There were a number of Congregational churches in the area, but we liked Cliff Town the best. Dr Trevor Davies was the minister then, but he left after only three years and was followed by

Bill Hodgkins, a very charismatic man. Under his leadership the church continued to flourish. There were guest preachers on Wednesday evenings and, during the summer months, his successor, Colin Garwood, held popular services at the bandstand. Bill's wife Lucy, now in her nineties, was the ideal minister's wife, and she lives in retirement in Cardiff.

Jean Wigley

An ancient church

Holy Trinity church, which I now attend, has a fascinating history. A wooden church was built on the site of Holy Trinity back in 824. There is no sign of that now, but there is documentation at Lambeth Palace that mentions the thane who gave the church and grounds to the Archbishops of Canterbury. Any rector considered for the church is appointed by the See of Canterbury, not by the Bishop of Chelmsford. Holy Trinity is the only church like that in the area. In the days of the wooden church there would have been clear land right down to the sea. The building was eventually burnt down and a stone church was put up on the site by the Normans. Late in the seventeenth century there were some renovations. Then a new section was built in 1906. The old church has now become the Lady chapel.

Ray Box

Romance under difficulties

I met my future wife through the church when she was nursing at Rochford Hospital. Sometimes the nurses came over to Prittlewell church. I went to the hospital when Canon Gowing, our vicar, took the sacrament there on a Monday morning. As a result of those visits I was invited to the nurses' Christmas dance. That was where I met Betty. Not long after that she was sent to Swindon to do her

Clockwise from top left:

Wesley Hall Methodist chapel is now the Southend mosque.

Jean and Tom Wigley in 1996.

The ancient church of Holy Trinity. (Reproduced by kind permission of the rector)

midwifery training, so we had to rely on letters for a while. However, when she came back she was the Night Sister and I was invited to the Sisters' Christmas dinner and dance. Then, when the war came, her family persuaded her to go back to Wales, so once again we had to rely on the post! When I had forty-eight-hour passes I hitch-hiked to visit her. We finally married in 1943 at St Mary's church, Prittlewell. There were no choirboys as they had been evacuated, but some of the remaining men choristers sang for us. We were worried that there might be a raid in the middle of the service, but luckily there wasn't, although on the first night of our honeymoon in Canterbury there were two raids! There was an anti-aircraft gun just round the corner that started popping away during the night.

Bernard Riley

The Dürer window in St Mary's church was removed for safety during the war.

Convent schooling

I went to St Helen's Roman Catholic School, which was the old building in North Road. The toilets were outside and there were big fireplaces in the classrooms. The fires were lit in the winter but there were bars round the outside to protect the children. When we got our socks and gloves wet we hung them on the bars to dry.

From there I moved on to St Bernard's School. It wasn't like walking into a school because the nuns were there then and it was like walking into their home. It had an aura about it.

Pamela Horsley

Protecting the stained glass

The beautiful stained-glass window from the Jesus chapel was removed from Prittlewell church during the war. It was hidden in the cellar of the old vicarage in West Street. It is a Dürer window dating back to the seventeenth century. Dürer was a well-known Flemish designer. The story goes that it was in the cathedral of Rouen and was taken out during the French Revolution. It was hidden away, but after the revolution was sold in pieces in the market place. Some ended up in Prittlewell church, four panels are in the West Window of St Peter's, South Weald and some even went to America.

Bernard Riley

West Leigh Baptist church

For as long as I can remember I have always been connected with West Leigh Baptist church, although my father belonged to the Boys' Brigade at Avenue Road Baptist church. Because there were other, smaller children in the family I was sent to the nearest church. That was West Leigh Baptist. I was taken at

West Leigh Baptist Church GLB members in costume in the 1940s. Beans are growing on the right, where there is now a car park.

The wedding of Frances Cutter and Reginald Winn at St Mary's church, Prittlewell, in 1930. Bob Winn is on the extreme left.

first, but after that I went on my own. That meant crossing the London Road which was always busy so I had to learn to be very careful. My mother belonged to Crowstone Congregational Church when she was a child. She was a member of 2nd Westcliff Girls' Life Brigade. I stayed at West Leigh Baptist church until after my marriage in 1962.

Over the years the building has been greatly extended. During the war what is now the car park was turned into allotments. We walked into church passing rows of beans. In the late 1950s a new church was planned and finally completed in the early 1960s. We were married in the new church.

Lois Holmes

Family connections

St Mary's church, Prittlewell, played an important part in the life of my family. My parents were married there in 1930 and the same vicar, Archdeacon Ellis Gowing, officiated at my own wedding twenty-eight years later. I was baptised there and so were my sister, Frances, and my brother, Clive. I went to the church school and was a member of the Sunday school and the Guides at one time. It's a beautiful old church with a real atmosphere.

Pamela Livingston

A supportive church

I was living with my family in Thorpe Bay and looking for a new church so we went to Holy Trinity, Southchurch. I liked the church, but I felt on the periphery of things.

Then my first wife became ill. I wasn't involved in any church work then. My wife didn't want any fuss, but when I knew that she only had a short time to live I told the rector, Canon Norwood. He was fantastic. He helped with the two children, looking after them after school. After that I became very much a part of the church and since my second marriage we have both been involved with all the various activities. We are on the PCC and together we became social care co-ordinators, looking after the social life of the parish and also its outreach. We are helped by a committee and plan fundraising events for the year and then run them. It is still a very flourishing church with an excellent musical tradition. At one time our choir sung at a number of cathedrals, allowing the regular choirs to have time off.

Ray Box

The Jesus Guild

The Jesus Guild was set up in Prittlewell in the Middle Ages. It was a religious guild and sort of the Social Service of the day. Members would bury corpses washed up on the beach. The Guild helped get apprenticeships for boys and found work for girls. They also took on the teaching of the children. This was done at the back of the church, behind the font, where there is a blocked-up doorway. It is said that it led through to a schoolroom.

The Jesus Guild was quite prosperous and it owned property. Then, with the dissolution of

Church socials were popular in the 1950s. This one is in St Marks' church hall. (Reproduced by kind permission of Echo Newspapers)

St Mary's Church, Prittlewell.

the monasteries of 1538, all the property was confiscated by the Crown and the Guild disappeared.

Canon Gowing decided to revive it. It was made up of communicant members of the church with a service to admit new members. There was a monthly service and the church was always pretty crowded. The Guild also ran bank holiday social outings to places like Cambridge and Canterbury. There were also evening dances. After the time of Archdeacon Gowing the Guild disbanded, but there is still the Jesus chapel in the church.

Bernard Riley

The old rectory

There is a very old part of Holy Trinity church and also a later addition. There used to be a large, old rectory with extensive grounds. It was sold some years ago after becoming derelict. It was developed and warden-controlled housing was built for old people. My mother, Annie Hall, was one of the first residents there. The old rectory itself was turned into flats.

Keith Hall

A church for life

A lot of my spare time was taken up with the church when I was a boy. I belonged to the choir at St Mary's Prittlewell. On Sundays I was at church morning, afternoon and evening, and then there was choir practise on Wednesday and Friday nights. You either belonged to the choir or Cubs. Our choirmaster was Mr Penny, who was very good, but strict. If you didn't behave you had to leave.

My week was organised around church activities, although on one night I visited the cinema and another I went out with the gang. On Saturday afternoon a group of us would go out for a bike ride. This was organised from the church and we might go to somewhere like Maldon. Then we would have a bottle of pop and a bun before coming back. There was a Children's Guild where there might be Magic Lantern slides. I started at Sunday school when I was five. In those days it met in the old school building. Then at eight I joined the choir and I stayed as a member until I reached ninety. At one point I learnt to play the organ and I also served on the PCC and became a server.

Bernard Riley

Jean and Tom Wigley with the Revd Bob Hoskins in 1955.

The Monkey Parade!

After I started work I often went to Cliff Town Congregational church with my friends in the summer. That was close to the bandstand, so we would go there after the service. It was where the girls congregated on Sunday evenings. It was known as the Monkey Parade as the youngsters walked up and down listening to the band and enjoying the evening.

Sydney Bridge

Ladies of the church

There were a number of ladies who were very active in St Mary's church. Nora Cable ran the Brownies and she was also a teacher at the school. She was a remarkable lady. Miss Wyman was a teacher there too, and then there were the Heal girls, Joy and Una; they were enthusiastic members of the church. There was a family called Watts. There were

two Watts boys in the choir and they always had a Christmas party, which I used to go to and so did the Heal girls. I've known them ever since.

Bernard Riley

Royal connections!

I went to the Manse one evening when Bill Hodgkins was at Cliff Town Congregational church. There I met Tom, who had recently been appointed to his own first church in Sailsworth, near Manchester. Some time later we were married at Cliff Town. The church looked magnificent with flowers arranged by Connie Fears, the local artist who worked for Longmans florist shop in Fenchurch Street and had been responsible for the Queen's wedding bouquet.

Jean Wigley

Ellis Gowing

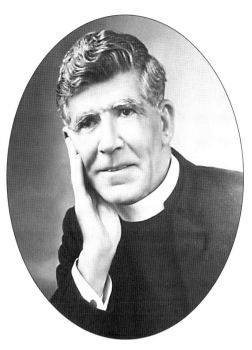

Archdeacon Ellis Gowing.

Canon Gowing had a great influence on my life. He came to England from Australia, and at first he worked at St James the Less, Bethnal Green. When the vicar, Dr John Watts Ditchfield, became the first Bishop of Chelmsford in 1914, he took Ellis Gowing with him as his domestic chaplain and Ellis later married the bishop's daughter, Dorothy. Ellis Gowing became the vicar of St Mary's, Prittlewell in 1917. He once told me that he was in trouble on his first Sunday in the parish because he didn't wear his top hat. Apparently the parishioners insisted that the vicar of Prittlewell church always wore a top hat to church on Sundays! He stayed as vicar until he died in 1960, by which time he was an archdeacon.

During his time at the church he was responsible for the establishment of St Luke's church when the housing estate was built. That was in about 1926. St Peter's was built when the Somerset Estate was being developed and then, after the war, St Stephen's was built in Manners Way to serve that area.

Leading up to the Second World War the parish thrived. That was when there were two evening services.

Canon Gowing was very proud of the school. When I was small only the old part of St Mary's School existed, and an earlier school had been built at the bottom of Prittlewell Hill. He always had all sorts of new ideas. Because it is a sacrament, there can't be collections at baptisms, but a collecting plate can be left near the door. Canon Gowing decided to keep that money on one side and, when there was enough, a window was put in close to the font and known as the Baptism Window. Later, he saved more money to put in another window that tells the history of the church. This includes a picture of the school at the bottom of the hill.

Bernard Riley

Accidental links

My links with St Mary's church, Prittlewell came about almost accidentally. I had an aunt who used to be in the choir at Chelmsford Avenue Congregational church. However, she was later confirmed at St Mary's. She was more like a cousin than an aunt because she was much younger than my mother. I started going to St Mary's with her. I already had a love for the old church and everyone respected the vicar, Canon Gowing. I remembered him from my time at school. On Sunday mornings the church would often be so full that extra seats had to be put at the end of each pew. One morning it was so full that I couldn't sit with my friend. He had to sit on a chair in the row in front. I must admit I really preferred the Church of England services to the nonconformist ones.

Sydney Bridge

5 Times of Conflict

Victoria Avenue and a First World War prison camp

In Victoria Avenue, south of Carnarvon Road, there used to be some very big houses. Next to my old school, Westcliff High, was a nice house with lovely grounds. It belonged to Sir William Dron, who was a Sheriff of the City of London. I saw how, when he was very ill, his wife had straw put all over the road to deaden the sound of the traffic going by.

My school stood where the civic centre is now. Before that was built the municipal buildings were scattered around the centre of the town.

The house used by Westcliff High School had been taken over as a prison camp for German officers during the First World War. When I went along Victoria Avenue by tram I could look down on the grounds of the camp. There was a high wall but it was possible to see the prisoners walking around as sentries patrolled.

Bernard Riley

Evacuation

Most of the schools in the town were evacuated in 1940 and mine was one of them. I went to St Mary's, Prittlewell. We had to leave from Prittlewell Station, wearing identity disks round our necks and carrying gas masks in little boxes over our shoulders. Clothes and other possessions were packed in small cases.

Apart from that we each had a child-sized haversack crammed full of food. There were sandwiches and small twists of paper containing currants and sultanas.

Our teachers had taught us to sing 'Goodbye mother, I must leave you' just before our departure. This we sung lustily on the station before the steam train arrived. I still remember the smell of that train.

My three-year-old sister, Frances, came along too and I, as a responsible six-year old, was expected to look after her! When we stopped at stations on the way people came and gave us sweets through the train window.

Pamela Livingston

Joining the RAF

I was seventeen when I left Holtby and Petty to join the RAF. I did various courses in this country, but I actually qualified as a navigator in South Africa, flying in a Lancaster Bomber. As a navigator I had a little cabin with a black curtain I could pull round so that no light escaped. We had what were called G Sets and these very sophisticated instruments had the name and Southend address of E.K Cole printed on them. So much for security!

I eventually left the Air Force in January 1947, just two weeks before I was due to marry at St Mary's church, Prittlewell. That was an anxious time, waiting for my release date to be posted.

Left: *Pamela Livingstone, left, with her sister Frances in 1939.*

Right: *Lois Holmes in 2003.*

Once I was a civilian again I returned to Southend. At that point, like so many others, I needed a job.

Frank Dudley

National Savings stamp

During the war everyone was encouraged to save and money for National Savings stamps was collected at school. I was given a ten-shilling note to take for stamps and somehow it disappeared. In those days ten shillings was a lot of money but fortunately my mother was very understanding and I wasn't smacked.

Lois Holmes

Black silk stockings

I must admit that I wanted to join the Wrens because I liked the uniform. There were no brass buttons to be cleaned and you wore black silk stockings. As soon as I was old enough I enlisted. However, that meant leaving Leigh and moving to Portsmouth. After leaving the Wrens I worked for a while in Shoebury for the Ministry of Defence.

Elvina Savill

Barrage balloons

Because I wasn't married I had to do war work. I was sent to work in a barrage balloon factory at Leigh Bridge Industries on the Southend Arterial Road. The two parts of the balloons were stitched together on a machine. One of my jobs was to stick the two sides together before they were stitched. We had to sit on the floor, put on the glue, flatten the material out and then stick the pieces together. Just one piece was left open where they could blow it up part way. Then someone went inside to test the seams.

Babs Haywood, left, working on a barrage balloon early in the war.

When we got on the bus to go home people moved away because we still carried a strong smell of the glue. I stayed there until they finished the quota of balloons, but some people were kept on to make inflatable dinghies.

Babs Haywood

Doodlebugs!

My parents were married at St Mary's church, Prittlewell in 1939, but when the war came they went to Wales where I was born. Dad was a boat builder and when we returned to Southend he worked as a carpenter and joiner for Adams Joinery in Prittlewell. I was three years old then and we lived in Surbiton Avenue in Southchurch. One of my first memories is

Mum saying, 'Doodlebug coming over!' I ran from the front to the back of the house to see the doodlebug. We thought if we kept moving the doodlebug wouldn't get us.

My dad belonged to the Home Guard. At that time we had a Morrison shelter inside the house. We dived under that when the air raids came.

John Horsley

Rationing

Sweets were a rare treat when we were children because of the rationing, but some cousins came from Canada once and they brought us boiled sweets and chewing gum. The butter ration was small, so we mixed it with mar-

Frank Bagnald in uniform, c. 1940.

two-up, two-down mill worker's cottage in Derbyshire. It had one tap in the kitchen; the front door led straight into the living room where there was one gas mantle and we had to take a candle to bed for light. The toilet was at the end of the block and it wasn't a flush one, but just a hole in the ground that went straight into the open sewer.

The first meal I had there was a real eye opener. The lady of the house asked if I liked chips. When I said I did, she peeled a potato, chopped it up and fried it on the open fire. Then she put the chips in a small dish and placed them in front of me. A little later she asked me what I was waiting for. 'Meat,' I told her. She looked at me in surprise. 'It's Tuesday. We don't have meat on Tuesday,' she said. She really wanted to have a boy, but later she was pleased to have me because my mother supplemented the money that the government paid her, so she looked forward to receiving her postal order each week.

Elvina Savill

Time spent in the Royal Air Force

When I was called up in 1942 I joined the Royal Air Force and trained as a ground wireless operator. By that time I was thirty-two, which was rather old for active service, especially as I wore glasses. I wasn't married then, but I did marry, in 1943.

Bernard Riley

garine in a big bowl using a large spoon.

Meat was also scarce. Once we were given three rabbits, which had hutches in the shed. There were three of us so we adopted one each and gave them names, but then one day when we came home from school there was a strange smell in the house and the hutches were empty. I have never eaten rabbit from that day to this!

Pamela Livingston

Chips for tea

Our house in Leigh was a modern three-bedroom semi with a bathroom upstairs, electricity, immersion heater, a kitchen downstairs and all the mod cons. I was evacuated to a

Wartime childhood

Although I wasn't evacuated during the war I was often sent to Gloucestershire where my grandparents lived. In fact, they were only eighteen miles from Bristol. On one occasion, the week I arrived, the city was heavily bombed.

Inside a barrage balloon examining seams.

I started school during the war and went to St Michael's, a private school run by the nuns. I was very happy there. At that time I walked across the fields to get to school, but now houses have been built in Eastwood Road. We learnt French at the school and all sung 'Frère Jacques'. We also had an end-of-term play. I was the farmer's wife in *Three Blind Mice* and had to run across the stage chasing my three friends who wore long tails.

I left St Michael's towards the end of the war and moved to West Leigh School. There were shelters dug out under the playground, and when the siren went we picked up our reading books or whatever we were doing, lined up and then made our way in complete silence to the shelter. The shelters were damp with the constant sound of dripping water and they had a strong, musty smell. There were small, flickering lights, but we were still expected to get on with our lessons. I was always terrified down there and I wonder how I ever learnt anything.

I was at the school when VE Day was celebrated. We had little rush mats in the play-ground and a local shop gave ice cream for all the children. That was the very first time I tasted ice cream.

Lois Holmes

Declaration of war

One Sunday morning in 1939 I went to church for the 9.30 a.m. service. We knew that an announcement about war was going to be made at 10 a.m. by the Prime Minister, Neville Chamberlain. I had a portable wireless set and the vicar, Canon Gowing, asked me to bring it along, go into the vestry and listen to the broadcast. The announcement came, 'From this moment this country is at war with Germany.' I went back into the church and told the vicar and he stopped the service and told the congregation that war had been declared. After the service, at twelve noon on that first morning, the siren went. Nothing happened, but it was quite a frightening experience.

Bernard Riley

A sheet metal worker

After leaving Leigh Bridge Industries I went to train as a sheet metal worker. Unfortunately, I picked up an infection from the metal, so I had to give up. In 1943, I joined the WAAFs and was told I could be a wireless operator or a cook. Well I didn't fancy being a cook so I became a wireless operator instead. I started training on my twenty-first birthday!

Babs Haywood

Join the Army, see the world!

I knew I would have to do National Service so I decided to enlist in the Army before I was called up. This meant signing on for three years. I did three years with the Colours and four on the Reserves. Enlisting gave me a considerable financial advantage. If you went in as a National Serviceman you were paid 28s per week, but as a Regular you got four guineas. I tried to sign on in the Brigade of Guards. Unfortunately I was rejected because of a slight impairment in one eye, although I didn't wear glasses until I was in my thirties! That was a disappointment because I used to ride a lot and hunt. Instead I went into Army Intelligence. To be honest I signed on for the pay, promotion and to see the world. In the end I didn't go anywhere. I was simply put in charge of training other soldiers. I was once on a plane for three days ready to go to Suez, but we didn't take off!

Ray Box

Barbed wire

During the war and immediately afterwards it was impossible to reach the beach at Southend. There was barbed wire and large concrete blocks, which had been put in place because of the fear of invasion. The first part of the beach to be opened up was at Chalkwell. We had to catch a train to get there but the beach was close to the station. Later we preferred going to Thorpe Bay by bus, because the beach there was quite good.

Keith Hall

Air-raid shelters

We had an Anderson shelter in our garden. One night the siren went and my mother called me but I always slept very heavily so I didn't move. I still have a vague recollection of her holding my twin brothers and somehow managing to drag me down the stairs too! Then we all had to go out into the garden to the shelter. We had bedding there, but the shelter started to flood and everything got very damp. Later we had a Morrison shelter which stood in the corner of the dining room,

A typical Anderson Shelter. (Frances Clamp)

but it was large and the room was small. It had a metal top, like a big table, and wire sides. Our bedding was put inside. At one time we also went under the stairs, but that must have been before we had a proper shelter. When the air raids were on we heard the drone of the planes going overhead.

One of our close neighbours was an air-raid warden and he knew that my dad was away, so he always walked up and down the road to see that everything was all right. Then he would knock on our door to see that we were all safe. On one occasion I put my head round the front door and saw the criss-cross of the searchlights going across the sky. That left a really vivid memory.

Lois Holmes

Call-up time

At one point the Territorials were called up. They came to a church parade and then they were marched off. Later all our choirboys went away when they were evacuated. In the end the choir consisted of men who were too old to be called up. You saw your friends going one by one as they were called up and then, after a time, some children began drifting back as we hadn't been invaded.

The pier became a naval establishment to supervise cargo ships going out. The convoys would assemble off the pier and you might see as many as a hundred with barrage balloons above to stop dive-bombers. By morning they would all have gone. Many of the larger houses along the seafront and the hotels above the cliffs were taken over by the military.

Bernard Riley

National Service

Eighteen-year-old males were expected to do National Service in the late 1940s and 1950s,

Keith Hall in RAF uniform in 1956, during his National Service.

and I went into the Air Force. At that time, when dressed in uniform, it was fairly easy to hitch-hike. I could get from Southend to Bury St Edmunds where I was stationed in about three hours on a Sunday evening. After basic training I discovered that many of my friends had acquired motorbikes and I bought myself a 250cc Panther.

Keith Hall

Bombed out!

In April 1940, during a German air raid, a land mine fell less than 200 yards from our house. As a result the back of the house was completely destroyed. We had an Anderson shelter in the garden, but it was always full of water so we moved downstairs to sleep. On that April night incendiary bombs were being dropped. Father watched from the front of the house and my mother went into the coal shed to get a galvanised bath which she intended to fill with water. I was in bed with my young sister.

When the bomb fell the French windows were blown in. As the glass from the leaded lights flew in I pulled the blankets over our heads, just as the full effect of the blast hit the house. That instinctive action almost certainly saved us from harm as the blanket absorbed all the glass splinters. However my mother, who was still in the garden shed, landed up on the gas stove in the kitchen, still holding the bath! The upstairs bath was found to be full of clumps of clay with daffodils still growing in them! There were more clumps throughout the house. The force had embedded strange things in the clay, like a knife and a comb. That night was the first one my mother had ever put my hair in rag curlers. I didn't let her do that again for months.

My father was bowled down the side way as all the slates fell from the roof and he was badly cut. Our next door neighbour was seriously cut too as she had been standing by the door. We learned later that two people had been killed in the explosion.

After that my mother picked us up and took us to our granny for the night. The following day father walked up the road and found an empty house. The blast had blown all the doors open so he walked in and commandeered it. Somebody came by and asked what he was doing in his brother's house and father said he would pay rent. So that's what happened and we stayed there for about two years until our house was rebuilt.

Elvina Savill

Shelters and air raids

Our Morrison shelter was kept in the front room and it was good for table tennis on the metal top. I wasn't evacuated but I did go to my grandfather's nursery at Rayleigh quite often. He had a lot of greenhouses heated by large boilers which had stoke holes that were used as shelters during air raids when the fires were out.

I remember the doodlebugs, or flying bombs. Once or twice when we were going to Rayleigh on the brown city bus we heard the engines cut out. Then you counted to ten, waiting for an explosion. My grandfather's nursery was hit by a land mine on one occasion.

Keith Hall

Women at war

When the war came I dearly wanted to join the Land Army, but I wasn't considered robust enough because I was small. Instead I went to work for E.K. Cole in Priory Crescent, the Ekco radio firm. From there we were evacuated to various parts of the country. I went to High Wycombe in Buckinghamshire, but I still worked for Ekco. Later we returned to Southend. At that time we made radios that were used in the Lancaster Bombers.

There was a fun side too. We had dances at the Ekco and it was at one of those that I met my future husband in 1945.

Audrey Dudley

Wartime ice cream

My school had an ice cream maker, even during the war. The ice cream was made with potato, but I thought it was gorgeous.

At home we didn't have an air-raid shelter. Instead we hid under the stairs. My mother pushed me in with my sister, but my parents stayed outside.

Diana Ayre

Above: *Leigh Bridge Industry workers during the war. (Photograph by Margaret Clark)*

Below: *Sydney Bridge in uniform during the Second World War.*

A soldier's return to Southend

In June 1940 the bombing raids started. My father had been told to leave Southend for health reasons and had moved to Dorset. By that time we had a three-month-old son. My parents suggested taking my wife and the baby with them. We felt it would be safer, so they went. I moved in with my wife's parents. Then a request was made to the local authority asking for volunteers to join the Royal Army Ordinance Corps. They wanted people with office experience, so I volunteered. I was accepted and joined up in October 1940. It was rather boring, but I stayed until I saw an advertisement for volunteers to join the Intelligence Corps. Applicants needed to be able to speak a European language other than French. I hadn't spoken German since leaving school so I was rather rusty when I did a test, but I was accepted.

I was posted to the north-west of England on the edge of the Lake District and was able to get my wife and son up there with me.

Then I was transferred overseas and on my first night on the boat we moored very close to Southend Pier.

Sydney Bridge

A cinema full of men!

One day during the war I visited the Corona cinema in Leigh. One of the Bob Hope 'Road' films was featured. When the lights went up it was a shock to discover that I was the only female civilian in the entire cinema. There was a sea of khaki.

Although the town was full of military personal I didn't have any problems throughout the whole of the war period. In fact life seemed much safer then. At home we never locked the back door.

The Methodist church ran a canteen for soldiers and I often helped. We sold them soap and cups of tea. The canteen ran for most of the war. Peggy Mount joined us from time to time as she lived in the area. On one occasion

she came to tell the pastor and his wife that, after being auditioned for the Court Players, she had just heard that she had got the job.

Elvina Savill

Under the stairs

One of my early memories is of living in Wenham Drive when, in 1916, an aircraft came over and searchlights lit up the sky. That was in the days before each family had a shelter and we used to crouch in the cupboard under the stairs. That was thought the safest place. Houses were sometimes taken over for billeting soldiers.

Bernard Riley

D-Day & VE Day

I went to a dance at the Kursaal Ballroom with a couple of soldiers who had taken part in the D-Day landings. They had been slightly

A Victory bonfire with Hitler on top, 1945.

wounded and had been sent to Southend for R and R. Leigh was a holding area before the lorries embarked for the D-Day landings. They had their exhaust systems extended to be above water level and were painted with a white circle round a white star. Some gardens were waist high in live ammunition boxes, regardless of whether or not there were children in the houses. There were also mobile ack-ack guns which were trailed around the town and fired from different positions.

The Kursaal Pleasure Ground was open and I went there on VE Day.

Elvina Savill

The end of the war

When the war ended my road, Flemming Crescent, wasn't made up, but Woodleigh Avenue was. There was land in Rayleigh Drive where we had a huge bonfire and Hitler's effigy was placed on top. Our party was in Woodleigh Avenue, where trestle tables were erected and as far as possible we wore something red, white and blue.

Lois Holmes

6 At Work

The borough treasurer's office

After taking the matriculation and spending a year at Pitmans' learning shorthand and typing I needed to look for work. My father wanted me to go into a bank and I saw a manager, but he didn't give me much encouragement. Instead I contacted my old headmaster and he said there was a job going in the borough treasurer's department and I should apply. As a result, I saw the borough accountant and got the job for £40 per year. That was in 1927 and I was appointed as a junior clerk. The office was in Alexandra Street.

Bernard Riley

Nine 'O' levels to stoke the boiler!

I took nine 'O' levels and then left school at sixteen. I would have liked to be a teacher, but I really needed to start earning and the careers officer suggested that I went into the bank instead. An uncle knew the manager at the Maldon branch of Barclays and, after an interview, I joined the bank. My first branch was in the Southend High Street, on the corner of Heygate Avenue, opposite the Odeon. It was the first time I wore a suit. I knocked gingerly on the front door and discovered that my first duty was to stoke up the boiler in the basement! I was also expected to walk around the office spraying disinfectant with a hand pump. I was there as a junior, making cups of tea, answering the phone, doing remittances and lugging big ledgers up and down the stairs. I left to do National Service at the age of eighteen.

Keith Hall

Nursing at Rochford Hospital

In 1932 I came from Wales to nurse at Rochford Hospital. People from Rochford visited the Welsh schools looking for possible nurses to come to England. My cousin went and so did two or three others. At first I had wanted to teach, but when my cousin came home she told me how lovely it was at Rochford Hospital and that there were lots of girls there from south Wales, I decided to join them.

When I think about those days now my early nursing experience was something of a sinecure, because we did nothing but the nursing. Our accommodation was catered for and we lived in the Nurses' Home for the first three months while we were on probation. Then we moved out into houses in Rochford because the Nurses' Home was quite small. Acacia House, at the top of the square, was also used. There were usually two or three nurses in a large room. It was very cold in the winter.

In South Street there was the night nurses' home where the night superintendent and a few staff nurses also lived. All the accommodation was very basic with a bed each and one dressing table between two. The pay was

Keith and Sally Hall in 2003.

Pamela Horsley in 2003.

terrible. I think it was about £20 the first year, but all pay was low then. There was an annual increment after the first year. In spite of that everything was provided, including our laundry and all meals.

Betty Riley

Holtby and Petty

In 1940 Southend High School was evacuated to the Midlands. At that time I was fifteen so I decided to look for a job. It was quite easy to get work at that time because so many people had left the town. Eighty thousand people were evacuated in one week.

I walked around on the first Saturday morning until I saw a notice saying 'Boy Wanted' in the window of an outfitters called Perhams'. I was interviewed by Mr Perham and he offered me the job for 12s 6d per week. This shop was on the corner of Milton Road and London Road.

On the way home along London Road I passed Holtby and Petty, a credit drapers' and outfitters'. They too were advertising for a boy but they were offering 15s per week. I went in, was interviewed and appointed to start on the Monday. Mr Perham understood when I explained. I used to sit at a big high desk, like Mr Pickwick and my job was to mark off in a book when people paid their weekly contributions. I stayed for three years until I volunteered to join the RAF.

Frank Dudley

A tight skirt and broken cups

I went to work as a clerk at Elmsleigh Engineering Company. I was feeling quite nervous and I was wearing a tight skirt and high heels. I worked upstairs in the office and went down to make the tea, carrying a tray of cups. The stairs came down to just outside the factory workshop. I missed my footing and ended up sprawled on the floor and surrounded by broken cups with all the factory workers laughing their heads off! I didn't feel I fitted in there after that.

Pamela Horsley

Southend Flying Club

I had originally been trained as a pilot at Stapleford Aerodrome in 1956. Later I became an instructor there before moving to Southend Airport in March 1968. That was when I started the Southend Light Aviation Centre, later to become Southend Flying Club. At that time I had two aeroplanes and operated the club from a caravan. Later the school became ever more successful until we had seven planes. There had once been a Municipal Flying School, but that had closed.

The school turned out to be highly successful and it's still running. In all I must have supervised around 100,000 flying hours and I personally flew 15,000 hours training people out of the airport. Many of those I taught are now flying in the major airlines, several as chief pilots. I suppose I trained around 1,000 qualified pilots to become flying instructors.

Edward Clack

A strange medical

I came to Southend with a friend at the end of August 1947. We were both teachers and I was offered a job at Westborough High School. Before starting I needed a medical and part of this was to step on and off the seat of a chair fifteen times! Apparently this proved that my heart was sound and I was appointed.

Anne Elliott

Suited for work

I left school and went to see the Youth Employment Officer and it was suggested that I either went into banking or insurance. My mother's only worry was that whatever the job it must carry a pension. I went to work for an insurance broker. Because I didn't have a suit I was sent off to Hamlet Court Road to buy

Edward Clack, seen here at the photographic window of a Cessna 152 aircraft.

one with money lent by the firm and it was then deducted from my salary. At first I earned 32s per week, and my mother took the whole amount, leaving me with sixpence per day. I first worked for a firm close to what is now the Cliffs Pavilion and I stayed there for two and a half years before joining the Army.

Ray Box

The rent collector calls!

I stayed in the borough treasurer's office for two or three years, until I heard of a job in the borough collector's office for £100 per year. There were also increments of £10. I applied and got the job. The office was on the opposite side of Alexandra Street and it was later absorbed into the borough treasurer's office. I stayed there and finally became chief cashier, which meant handling cash, because there were no credits or direct payments at that time. All the cash had to be paid into the bank every day.

We collected rents, rates, mortgage payments – in fact any money that was due to be paid to the Corporation. We sent out rent collectors to the big Corporation estates in areas like Sutton Road and Manchester Drive. I did my share of rent collecting too. The rents at that time were around 16s a week, but some in Sutton Road were £1 3d. We would collect around £100 in a morning. In the afternoon, after paying in the cash and making up the books, we settled down to our more routine work. When the war started, being in local government, I was in a reserved occupation. However, in 1942 I was finally called up.

Bernard Riley

Hazards of steam travel

When I started work I travelled to London each day by steam train and on one occasion I was going out to a dinner dance. My dress was

Bernard Riley in 2003.

of black and white taffeta. The carriage window was open, and suddenly a spark flew in and the next thing I knew there was a smell of burning and a hole in my dress!

Diana Ayre

From Box Brownie to aerial photography

I'd always been interested in photography, ever since I borrowed a Box Brownie from my Aunty Gladys in 1935. I've still got that camera, and my first photographs taken on a school trip. I joined the RAF in 1942 and became a reconnaissance photographer, flying as crew. Even then I knew that one day I wanted to become a pilot. Many of the photographs I shot then were taken over Iraq and the Gulf.

Since those days, and especially since starting the flying school, I've taken thousands of aerial photographs. Quite a number of these

Woolworths in Southend High Street.

have been used in my own books and also in other people's.

Edward Clack

Woolworths

I was born in 1910 and, after leaving school, I became a trainee manager at Woolworths. For some time I worked in the Chelmsford branch, but then I was sent to Southend to help out during the holiday season. This often happened if one store became extremely busy and, being a seaside town, Southend faced this problem every summer.

We were expected to work very long hours. I would start at 8 a.m. and very often I didn't finish until 8 p.m. This was for a six-day week.

During that time I lived in digs in the last house in Alexandra Street, which ran along beside the shop. The Rivoli Cinema was in the same road and it was quite close to the bandstand.

On one occasion there was a landslide on top of the cliffs and my wife was injured. My wife worked for Woolworths, as a cashier. That was where we met.

Jack Kendal

Up to London

After leaving Westcliff High School I did a secretarial course and then got my first job working for the Nuffield Foundation in London. That meant travelling from Southend Victoria station each day. I don't think I realised at the time just how dirty and smelly those journeys were. You were expected to wear a hat for work in those days. Later I took a job in Southend with an estate agent. The firm was called Acock and Son. Mrs Acock was in charge and her son also worked there, and Mr Frank Sparrow.

Pamela Livingston

Return from the Army

After leaving the Army I returned to my old job in insurance in Southend. I married when I was twenty-one at St Mary's church, Prittlewell. The trouble was that on leaving the Army my salary dropped from £20 per week to £7. When I told my employer that I wanted to get married and I needed more money he told me that they didn't expect their employees to marry before they were twenty-five! However, I was offered an annual increase of £50! I stayed for another six months, but after that I was promoted to London. For the next forty years I travelled up each day by rail, the first eight years on steam trains.

Ray Box

Babs and Dennis Haywood in 2003.

The chippy

My first job after leaving school was with Barhams in Fairfax Drive. I was paid 1s 1d by the hour. That was for working as a wood machinist on the end of a machine that was cutting flooring. I lifted and stacked the cut wood. I stayed there a year before moving to Goodwins' shopfitters in Rochford Road.

Next I moved to Sunny Dawes for 5s an hour. Sunny was the father but I worked for his son, Tom, whose sister also worked there. I was coach building at that time and I continued as a coach builder when I later moved to RTS. After that I worked with my dad for some years as a carpenter and joiner.

In 1975 most of the Kursaal site was knocked down. I was there for a couple of years as a steel fixer and the summer of 1976 was so hot we worked in our underpants! I earned a lot more than I did with my dad, but I wasn't using my woodworking skills.

John Horsley

A new bike

Fourteen was school leaving age so that was when I had to find my first job. I worked for Mr Bignell, who ran a leather and hardware shop opposite Nazareth House. We sold nails by weight and we cut the leather by hand with a very sharp knife. I worked in the shop, but I spent quite a lot of time helping his wife because she was very ill. She was also a very kind lady. One day I told her about a bike I'd seen in a shop, for which they wanted a half-crown deposit. She said she would give it to me, but later I discovered that she had paid for the whole bike.

Babs Haywood

The depression

The year 1930, when I left school, was a period of depression. The question of what

Dating from the late thirteenth century, Southchurch Hall was a library for many years.

you wanted to do wasn't really relevant. I applied for a job at Barclays Bank, but they didn't take on anyone until they were seventeen. I then applied to another bank, who interviewed me and also my father. I was offered a job, but only if my father transferred his account from Barclays. I refused to take the job under those conditions.

I was finally offered a job with a London insurance company, but one of the conditions was that I must join the Territorial Army. I had no wish to do that so I decided to work with my father, who was a farmer. Then a letter came from Mr Williams, the headmaster of Westcliff High School. It said that he had been asked to recommend someone for the Southend Libraries Department and he wondered if I would be interested. Of course, I was extremely interested, so I went for an interview. Some time before that I had been on a school holiday to France. We had visited Les Eyzies, where the cave drawings are, and

were allowed to do some digging there. I talked about this during the interview and as the job included working at the Prittlewell Priory Museum they decided that I would be suitable and I was duly appointed.

Sydney Bridge

Drought!

In 1922 there was a drought. This was a difficult time on our smallholding so my father took a job driving for a coach company. He would go up to London, collect a group, and then bring them down to Southend. Then he would take them to the Rose Tea Garden at Barling or to the Exhibition Inn at Wakering and then he would drive them back again at night. In the meantime our mother looked after things at the smallholding.

Frank Bagnald

Work at Melrose, home of the Bagnald family.

Pots of money

When visiting the pier for pleasure it was usual to walk to the end and then take the train back, but when I was in the borough treasurer's office it was different. I had to go out to pay the Corporation staff. Cashiers had to go to the parks, along the seafront to pay the foreshore staff and then down the pier by train. We would stop at the signal box at each end to give the signalmen their pay. In those days there was a double track. Before the war the money was made up in little tins, each with a number; the worker would say his number and the money would then be tipped out into his hands. At that time the wage was likely to be under £3. The 10s notes and the pounds would be folded up with any odd coins, but later small envelopes were used. There were fewer people by then but they were paid much more.

Bernard Riley

Teaching in the 1950s

At first I worked in the borough treasurer's office, but later I left office work and went away to Avery Hill Teachers' Training College, which was a residential college.

On my return to Southend I worked briefly at Wentworth High School and then moved to Westborough High School, which I loved. My classroom was away from the main building, in an annex, and to reach this wing you had to pass through the junior and infant school playgrounds.

The younger children's playtime was at a different time from the seniors and they were warned not to come near our building. However, occasionally they strayed. My room had a door at the back and on one memorable occasion I had a class full of thirty-five children. It was impossible to teach when playtime was in progress, so my pupils were working quietly. Suddenly a little figure burst in through the back door, came right up one of the aisles and yelled at the top of her voice, 'Knickers!' For a few moments there was stunned silence. Then the class burst out laughing and the little mite turned tail and fled back the way she had come. The lesson didn't really get back on course again after that!

Pamela Bissell

The Rothmans bus

In the 1970s, Rothmans, the cigarette company, wanted a bus converted and fitted out for the air show on the seafront. Somebody asked if I'd like to go to Grays to work on the Rothmans bus. That meant coach building

Above: *Westborough High School, built in 1911.*

Right: *The Rothmans' bus after conversion.*

and carpentry again. They wanted it finished in three weeks, so sometimes it meant working all night, but we got it done in time. Then it came down to Southend and cigarettes were sold from the side of the bus. After that I worked on converting other buses for export to Hong Kong.

John Horsley

Night sister

After I was fully qualified, Matron asked if I would return to Rochford Hospital as night sister in charge of midwifery. New mothers always stayed in hospital for ten days then. I agreed, but when the war came my mother thought every bomb had my name on it and she wanted me back in Wales, so I carried on nursing in Monmouthshire. However, by that time I had met my future husband and after we were married I returned once more to Southend.

Betty Riley

Frank Bagnald in 2003.

Return to Civvy Street

After the war I went back to the Gas Light and Coke Company in York Road. All the gas mains were relaid when Basildon was developed and natural gas came in. Then in 1960 I joined Lloyds Bank and I stayed with the bank until I retired. I finished my time at the Hamlet Court Road branch. The building has now become an Italian restaurant.

Dennis Haywood

A strange coincidence

I took my preliminary library examinations and later became main branch librarian at Southchurch. In 1938 I passed the intermediate exams, which meant that I could put ALA after my name. Not long after that I became branch librarian at Leigh and it was during my time there that I married. For a time we lived in Leigh. When I told the deputy librarian that I was getting married he said he hoped I had better luck than he had, because exactly two months to the day after his wedding the First World War was declared. Strangely enough, exactly two months to the day after I was married the Second World War was declared!

Sydney Bridge

Driving in the dark

After finishing at Art School I went to work at Cramphorns'. I was in the shop dealing with the plants, but later I moved from there and

Lloyds Bank in Hamlet Court Road is now an Italian restaurant.

went to work for Mr Todd-Reave, a well known local dentist.

Then the war came. My father had decided by that time to go back into pork butchery and he had the chance to acquire a pork butcher's shop at the top of the steps in Leigh. Under his care this became well known for its pork pies. Before that he and my brother Frank had been pig breeders and slaughter-men. There was a slaughterhouse at Melrose, which linked nicely with the new shop. At that point my brother went into the forces so, while my father ran the shop, my mother and I looked after the smallholding. I drove a large van and took my father to work early each morning, using blinkered headlights because of the wartime regulations.

Rhoda Deane

After the war

It was a condition of my employment that, if I wanted to return to my old job after the war, then I could do so. My salary had been made up by the council while I was away, so I had to inform the authority if I got promotion so that the money could be adjusted. Not all employers did that, but the local Corporation did. During the war the officer who I had succeeded at Leigh Library, Alfred Cranfield, was excluded from military service on medical grounds. He decided not to finish his final library examinations because that would give him an unfair advantage over those who were away. Then he suddenly decided to give up library work and go into teaching. When I came back there was a vacancy in the Central Lending Library as chief assistant. I was

Barclays Bank on the corner of Hamlet Court Road and London Road.

appointed because I had already passed my intermediate examinations, which meant that I was qualified for the post. Then I went to the City of London College for a year to take my finals. That was with a government grant. After passing the final exam there was a thesis to be completed, which was interesting because it meant going to the British Museum to study old books there.

After I was qualified the deputy librarian retired and I was appointed in his place and I stayed in that job until I retired.

Sydney Bridge

A life on the move in banking

After National Service I returned to Barclays Bank. A flat became available over the branch on the corner of Hamlet Court Road and the London Road. It was a typical solid-looking bank building and the 'flat' was three stories high with huge rooms and an iron staircase at the back. The rent was extremely reasonable. There was a very small garden at the back so we couldn't do much gardening. Anyway, we put up a large shed which was very useful as it held the pram after our son, Andrew, was born.

I worked in Leigh for a time and then briefly in Hamlet Court Road. After several bank moves we bought our first house in Carlton Avenue. A three-bedroom semi cost the princely sum of £2,400 in the early 1960s. I moved around Essex fairly frequently with the bank, going to Billericay as chief clerk and later to Braintree as assistant manager. At that point we moved to Great Baddow so that I could get to work and Sally could travel back to Southend for her various sports commitments. When I transferred to Chelmsford we moved back to Hadleigh.

Keith Hall

7 At Play

The Kursaal

When I first started working many of my friends went to dances at the Kursaal ballroom. On one occasion I went to the Kursaal fairground when one of my cousins came to visit. Once there we saw the Wall of Death rider, Tornado Smith. He spent his time going around in circles up and down the wall on a motorbike, which was incredibly noisy. The act was really brilliant. There were some very big rides, including a water shoot and a huge frame holding torpedoes where you shot round on long arms. They went up and down and sometimes you stayed in the air upside down. I didn't venture on most of the rides, but I did go on the Caterpillar. This just went up and down and a lid came on and off as you went around. Most of that area has now been cleared and turned into a housing estate.

Pamela Bissell

Auditioning for the Leigh Operatic Society

The first thing I faced when I wanted to join Leigh Operatic Society was an audition. That was extremely daunting as I'd never done anything like it before. I took along my own piece of music to sing, which was then given to the pianist. As we hadn't previously met, there was no chance of practising together. A panel of six people listened and then I was asked what I'd done before. My previous experience had been in Gang Shows during my scouting days.

After that the choreographer came and showed me a few steps, which I then had to copy. Next I was given a passage from a script to read, and I had to take the part of one of the characters. Presumably this was to find out if I had any speech problems. At the end of that hair-raising session I was told they would let me know! In fact that wasn't too bad because I heard that I'd been accepted within a week.

Chris Sawford

Outings to the Odeon

The Odeon in Southend High Street was an amazing building. The first time I ever went there was with the school to see *Coppélia*, performed I believe by the Royal Ballet Company. Many well-known personalities appeared there. On one occasion there was a harmonica player, who threw out miniature harmonicas into the audience. By that time I had three brothers and one sister, so with my parents we took up quite a large part of the front row and we ended up with three harmonicas!

Harry Worth also appeared there and so did Laurel and Hardy. One of my friends wrote to Stan Laurel before the performance because her surname was Jefferson and so was his. She was invited backstage as a result of her letter.

Lois Holmes

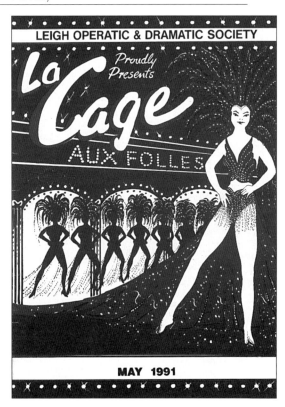

Chris Sawford was one of the performers in La Cage Aux Folles.

Cinemas

Southend had a huge number of cinemas when I was young. There was the Garrison at Shoebury and the Plaza in Southchurch Road. The Talza stood at the end of the arcade of that name at Victoria Circus and on the other side of the road was the Gaumont. That had previously been called the Hippodrome. The Cinema Delux stood close to Dixons, but that was burnt down. There was also the Strand and, in the High Street, the Odeon and Garons. In the interval Garons had fountains that came up and were lit in ever changing colours and an organ played. The Odeon had an organ too, which later went to Rochford Hospital.

Just off the High Street there was the Rivoli and the Ritz. There was also the Lyric in Tylers Avenue and a theatre called the Regal.

Following the London Road towards Leigh there was King's Hall in Hamlet Court Road, The Mascot and also the Metropole at Westcliff. The latter was built after the others and later became known as The Essoldo. To reach the front you had to go up a number of steps. In Leigh there was the Corona, the Coliseum and the Empire. Hadleigh had the Kingsway, and behind the Blue Boar in West Street there was a cinema called Gibbs.

Frank Bagnald

Carnival

Carnival was an amazing time. In the 1950s the whole town hummed. Everywhere was busy and to get a good place to watch the procession you had to claim your position very early in the morning. It was really exciting

The Children's Carnival Fancy Dress Show, seen here in around 1972, was always popular.

and the way the floats were decorated was fantastic. It all started with the choosing of the Carnival Queen. Photographs of the entrants were put in the Southend Standard and then the selection of the queen and her court took place at the Odeon. As well as the Saturday procession there was a Wednesday one and a torchlight procession.

The fête in Chalkwell Park lasted for a whole week, with rides and raffles and lots of noise! The whole thing was run by the Carnival Association. It is more commercialised and expensive now. The Scouts put a float in the procession with the help of Norman Garon, who let us build it in his yard and garage. We built a rocket and the boys dressed up as spacemen.

The lights were switched on during Carnival Week and there was also the Guiness Clock along the seafront. That did all sorts of amazing things and all the Guiness signs were there, including the toucan.

Doreen Sawford

The Lindisfarne Players

The Lindisfarne Players rehearsed at the old Lindisfarne Roman Catholic School in Valkyrie Road. Part of the building became a banqueting suite and we hired a couple of rooms for rehearsals. Usually we performed at St Bernards, but on one occasion we took part in a festival for amateur players. This was at the Palace Theatre. Our play was called *The Rag Woman of the Shambles*. It was set in the eighteenth century and right at the end I got murdered. Our second daughter started crying because she thought I'd really been killed!

Pamela Horsley

Sunday night at the Kursaal

We used to go along to the Kursaal on a Sunday night. Dad would be home then and sometimes we went on the Water Shoot. Then there was a greyhound racing game. You wanted your dog to reach the winning post first. There was a helter-skelter, but the coconut mats were very rough. One of the things we liked best was the woman in a bed. You had to throw something and if you scored then the woman fell out.

John Horsley

Television programmes and ballet lessons

In the late 1960s I watched *The Persuaders* on my friend Martin Ballard's television. Although he only lived around the corner in Rayleigh Road they could get Anglia Television on their set and we couldn't in Snakes Lane. Sometimes Dad took me for walks with my friend Maxine Bird across the fields close to the airport, which was a long walk for little legs. There were fields pretty well all the way from Eastwood to Rochford, but that has all changed now. The road has been straightened and there are lots of houses and commercial buildings.

I went to ballet lessons in Leigh, held in St Clements church hall. Miss Carol Strutt was the teacher and her sister played the piano. Once a year we put on a show, and one year we did an Easter bonnet parade. My mother could make anything out of crêpe paper and so I had the most wonderful crêpe paper bonnet.

Mary Wigley

Southend Boys' Choir

Madam Freda Parry ran a boys' choir in the town and I became a member and a soloist. She was very strict. We used to do *Sunday Half Hour* for the radio, making the recording at the Pier Pavilion. Unfortunately I had to leave because there was a conflict of interest between my church choir and Southend Boys' Choir.

Ray Box

Times of change

I joined St Georges Presbyterian church when I first came to Southend. However, being involved with Sea Rangers left very little time for me to attend the church as we often rowed, sailed or worked on the boat on Sundays. Things were changing. We joined up with the Senior Scouts to form Clarendon, the first mixed Unit to be registered at Scout Headquarters. We met at the scout hut in Old Leigh. We also camped at Belchamps, went for overnight walks and some members even tackled the Pennine Way.

Anne Elliott

Performing at the Palace

A show lasts for a week. Before a performance there are always some butterflies, but it's worse if you're in a lead role. Before the curtain rises there are various announcements made over the tannoy directly into the dressing rooms. First the orchestra is told to go to the pit. Next, beginners in Act one have to go to the side of the stage. It is then, as the curtain goes up, that the adrenaline kicks in and all those months of working together as a cast begin to pay off. Most performances are out of normal work time, although it may be necessary to take time off for the Wednesday matinee.

The most exciting show I have been in was *La Cage Aux Folles*, which was all about a transvestite nightclub. The most difficult part about this production was learning to tap dance in high heels and to walk like a woman – not the easiest thing to do.

Ready for the Easter bonnet parade, c. 1966.

Gentlemen of the cast onstage at the Palace Theatre.

Once there was the Little Theatre Club and also the Westcliff, Southend, and Leigh Operatic Societies, but some have now closed because of the high production costs.

The Palace Theatre is now being used for shows again. We had to move for a while when the theatre closed, but the Palace is a friendly theatre and it is an excellent place to perform and to see local amateur productions.

Chris Sawford

Married to the scoutmaster

We were engaged and had the opportunity to rent a bank flat in Hamlet Court Road. That was in St Saviour's Parish so that was where we were married. Later my husband became the scoutmaster there.

Sally Hall

The Hippodrome

The Hippodrome was a music hall. It stood in Southchurch Road, next to the Victoria Hotel, which was very posh. It had a covered way from the High Street so that those staying there could go straight from the street inside without getting wet on rainy days. Later the Hippodrome became the Gaumont cinema. That was when music hall was losing its popularity. When it was still a theatre we used to queue to go up in the gods, which cost about sixpence. When they opened the doors the first call was, 'Early doors' and people could pay extra to go in first. Then the rest followed. Up there you sat on wooden boards, and from this great height I looked down on the plush seats in the pit – it was my ambition to be rich enough one day to sit there. There were two houses each night.

Bernard Riley

Concerts

The Odeon was the largest cinema in the town, and it doubled up as a concert hall at times. I heard Gigli sing there. The building was close to the railway and, during one quiet passage, I heard a train passing. That was also the place where I first saw live ballet. Some of the concerts were excellent and later there were good concerts at the Plaza too. The Plaza was at one time a small cinema, but it has now been completely revamped and is rather splendid.

The town had many cinemas including the Rivoli in Southend. The Rivoli is now being refurbished and used for some live entertainment. It's possible to be shown round the old cinema and to visit parts that go back to the 1950s. Some graffiti was found on one wall mentioning bombs and at first this was thought to refer to the Second World War, but apparently it is now believed to date back to the First World War.

Pamela Bissell

The Pom-Pom concert party

Mr Knivitt from Olivier Drive started the Pom-Pom concert party and his wife made the costumes. I was a contralto, Frances Winn was the soprano with Reg Winn as the comedian and Frank Clements was also a member of the group. Mr and Mrs Knivitt's daughter Dorothy was the dancer. We went around giving concerts for charity, visiting a number of churches and also the Rochford Workhouse. The group finally folded shortly before the war. One year we had a float in the Southend Carnival and my father gave some plums to distribute to those watching.

Rhoda Deane

Rhoda Deane (née Bagnald) ready to perform in The Jewel Of Persia *in 1925.*

Film censorship

When I first came to Southend in 1959 I became a member of the Conservative Party. Then, in 1968, I was invited to let my name go forward as a candidate for a council by-election and I was duly elected. This was in Victoria Ward, where we were living.

At that time I was still working in London, but I managed to fit my council work around my job. I took over the vacancies left by my predecessor on the council, including the Education Committee and the Watch Committee, which became Public Protection. Among other tasks, Public Protection involved vetting films that might have been considered unsuitable to be shown in the town! We went on Saturday mornings to one of the local cinemas, although I think we only rejected one film during my time on the committee.

Geoffrey Ayre

The Eastwood Evening Townswomen's Guild

It is now over forty years since I first joined the Townswomen's Guild. In that time I have done every job except treasurer and twice served as chairman.

There was a time when the Eastwood Evening Guild became so popular that there had to be a waiting list. Sadly those days have gone.

There is also a South East Essex Federation of Townswomen's Guilds and I became a representative, a committee member and later the chairman. There is also a National Union of Townswomen's Guilds and they have an annual meeting. It used to be held at venues all round the country and some people treated it as their main holiday. Nowadays it is usually held in the Royal Albert Hall, but sometimes we still travel further afield.

Maureen Ollett

Maureen Ollett (front right) at the Royal Albert Hall for the TWG annual conference.

Prittlewell's cinema

We had our own cinema in Prittlewell when I was a boy, behind the Blue Boar. It was originally called the Priory and had various name changes including Gibbs' Cinema, the Gaiety and the Star.

Sydney Bridge

Cubs

My eldest son, Christopher, started in Cubs when he was eight. I had always wanted to get him into scouting because I thought it was such a good thing. There was a vacancy at 1st Prittlewell, St Mary's pack, so he joined. One day he came home and said they wanted help with test work and he had volunteered me! I went along and before too long ended up as Akela. We met in the church hall and the people who helped me were Miss Cable, who ran the Brownies and also taught at the school, and George Stacey, Group Scout Leader.

I stayed as Akela for the next sixteen years. We camped and attended monthly church parades. At meetings we played games, did badge work and took part in sports activities. I always had a full pack of thirty-six boys. I have lots of happy memories of that time and I still meet many of the boys who now have children of their own. Now my eldest grandson, Myles, has joined the same pack. Pat Webb, who used to help as my assistant, has become the Akela.

Doreen Sawford

A local comedian

Chelmsford Avenue Church Choir, to which my parents belonged, used to go out to the surrounding villages in winter to give concerts. I went along too and Reg Winn often joined us. He was a comedian and he would tell jokes and sing a song. I quite hero-worshipped him in those days. This would have been some time before 1926. On concert nights I went to bed a bit later than usual, but not that late because I think we all went to bed earlier in those days.

Sydney Bridge

Reg Winn at the rear and friends, c. 1929.

Shorty bottoms and flaky tops!

One of the first committee meetings I went to for the Townswomen's Guild seemed to consist of a very long discussion on whether the Christmas mince pies should have 'shorty bottoms and flaky tops'. My friend and I hadn't the faintest idea that they were talking about pastry! Apparently food was always important to members. Back in 1949, a food licence had to come from the Food Office for organisations offering refreshments. Permits were still needed in 1951 and in that year permission had to be granted for dried egg to be obtained to make the cakes. The person making the application had to be specially registered.

Maureen Ollett

Playing in the band

I used to play the piano accordion in a dance band before the war. One night I was playing in the British Legion Hall in Victoria Avenue when I met Babs, my future wife. The hall had been opened by Queen Elizabeth, later the Queen Mother. I also played at the Masonic Hall, at Garons in the High Street and at the Palace Hotel.

I worked in the accounts department of the Gas Light and Coke Company on the seafront and in the evening I played in dance bands. When the war came I was in a reserved occupation, but I volunteered for aircrew and joined up in 1943.

In 1945, after the war, we were married at St Saviours' church. Babs wore a borrowed dress because clothes were still on coupons and my new mother-in-law managed to do the catering, despite the rationing. Once we

Dennis Haywood, standing with the piano accordian, playing with the dance band.

were married Babs could leave the WAAFs and I was finally demobbed in 1947.

Dennis Haywood

Floats

As a teenager, I often came to Southend on summer weekend afternoons. We bought a special cheap train ticket, and a group of us would come and then stay on in the evening for the lights. We usually got off at Chalkwell and then worked our way along towards Southend.

I later got involved in the carnival through the Townswomen's Guild. Someone suggested that we should apply to the Carnival Committee so that we would be allocated a float. We were accepted and the first year we went as nursery rhyme characters. The float was completely covered with crêpe paper flowers. Another year we went as the Gnomes of Eastwood and once we had a giant globe and flags. Henry VIII and his wives was another theme and we also covered a float with bras one year in support of BUST, Lady McAdden's charity. This supported a clinic for detecting breast cancer. The initiative to build the clinic came first from Norma Heigho, a keen local TWG member. Later we didn't have a float, but we decorated a pram in the Guild colours of red, white and green and pushed that in the procession.

Often we would watch the procession with our children from the cliffs. You could see everything from there.

Maureen Ollett

Time out of school

As a child I used to go to the Saturday morning cinema club at the Odeon in the High Street. There were lots of cartoons and some black and white films. It was incredibly noisy.

I also joined the Sunday school and Cubs at St Mary's church. I became pack leader and later went into the Scouts. This meant that there was

Above: *Eastwood TWG members with their decorated carnival pram.*

Right: *Boy Scout membership card, issued in 1948.*

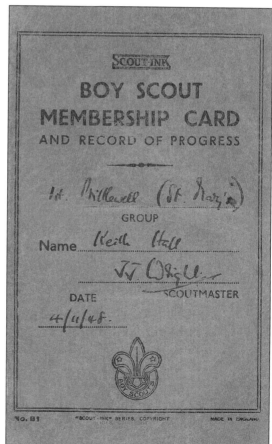

plenty of camping and weekends away. It took up a large part of my life at that time.

Keith Hall

Beauty and the Beast

My sister made a monster's head at school and we decided to use it in the carnival procession and go as Beauty and the Beast. The procession always took place on a Saturday afternoon towards the end of August, but the whole week was given over to fund-raising events and there was a huge fair in Chalkwell Park. The day of the procession was very hot. I dressed up as Beauty and my sister, who had made a green costume to go with her head, went as the beast. We walked the whole way from Leigh to Southchurch with our collecting boxes getting heavier by the minute. I don't know how much we collected, but most of it was in the large old pennies.

Pamela Livingston

Working at Shell Haven

I moved to Southend in 1958 when I got a job at Shell Haven. That was shortly before we got married. At first I travelled by bus, but later we got our own transport. We had a flat in West Road behind a radio shop, but later we moved to Wenham Drive and that's where we brought up our family.

We lived not far from the Palace Theatre so we went there quite often. Then, when our eldest son joined Leigh Operatic Society, we became more interested in the theatre. The Odeon was always the place to see big stars – we saw the Rolling Stones there, Ella Fitzgerald and Billy J. Kramer. These were mainly Sunday concerts, because it was used as a cinema during the week. This was in the days before the Cliffs Pavilion was completed.

Bill Sawford

Patches

I've always been very keen on needlework and dressmaking, and it became my career. After getting my City and Guilds certificate I trained as a teacher and worked in a Southend school. One day someone at the Townswomen's Guild suggested that we should have a patchwork class, so I started one up. We all brought along scraps of material and made a quilt and it was finally raffled in aid of the Fairhavens Hospice. That really sparked off my interest in patchwork. From then on I studied more about the subject and later I found out about the Quilters' Guild which I joined. Then I discovered that there were a lot of people in Southend who were interested in patchwork, so we formed our own group. It needed a name and we wanted one that said something about the town. There were many suggestions but we finally settled on 'Pier Patchers'. We are on the list of organisations in the town. A journalist from a local paper telephoned one day to say that he wrote special interest pieces about the town's various groups. He said our Pier Patchers intrigued him, but what he wanted to know was how we patched the pier! He was quite disappointed when he learnt the truth.

Maureen Ollett

Gang Shows

The Cubs weren't involved in the Gang Shows, but the Druid Venture Scouts were. The Druids used to do shows for the elderly at the Carnarvon College and they also did charity concerts. The South East Essex College was where they did quite a lot of their shows and there was also the Southend Gang Show at the Palace Theatre. Ralph Reader started it all and he once came to one of the Druid shows.

Doreen Sawford

PALACE
THEATRE
WESTCLIFF

SOUTHEND-on-SEA
GIRL GUIDES and
BOY SCOUTS

present

IT'S A
DATE
1966

PROGRAMME
ONE SHILLING

Clockwise from top:

TWG patchwork group members' display their quilt in 1987. It was later raffled in aid of Fairhavens Hospice.

Pamela Livingston, left, and her sister Frances as Beauty and the Beast in 1952.

Scouts and Guides perform in 1966.

8 Active Lives

Southend United at the Kursaal

To get into the Kursaal football ground we had to walk under the Water Shoot. There was one notable centre forward named Billy Hick. He regularly aimed at the goal, but often sent the ball over the Water Shoot!

When she was a girl the wife of one of my cousins went to watch Southend United at the Kursaal. She and her father had season tickets. In the south-east corner of the ground there was a tiny stand where she used to watch the matches, and behind that were the dressing rooms. The players had to go in and out through that corner of the ground.

Sydney Bridge

Boys on one side, girls on the other

I went to the Stansted School of Dancing as a teenager. We were rather shy and girls sat on one side of the room and boys on the other, but we learnt to do waltzes and quicksteps when we occasionally met up in the middle. Later, while I was on leave from basic training in the RAF, I went to an old time dance at Westcliff High School and that was where I met Sally, my future wife.

Keith Hall

Tennis

The houses of the smallholdings in Prince Avenue were built in pairs. One of the smallholdings had a tennis court and we had a tennis club there called the Glenwood Club. It belonged to the Patrick family and was an official club because we used to play in a league in inter-club matches. There was a hut and Mrs Patrick made the teas, and for some reason we always had Marmite and watercress sandwiches.

Rhoda Deane

Scouting

Briefly, I belonged to St Mary's Men's Club where I played snooker. I think my real interest in sport started after meeting my future wife. She was very keen on tennis and badminton. I joined Westcliff Lawn Tennis Club and Leighway Badminton Club.

I left the Scout troop at St Mary's at the age of sixteen as there was no senior Scout group, but after we were married in 1959 I became an assistant Scoutmaster at St Saviour's church and later became Scout Leader. I continued in scouting for the next ten years, but then gave it up to concentrate on the banking exams.

Keith Hall

Right: *Rhoda Deane in 2003.*

Below: *Scouts at Belchamps ready to start cooking in around 1969. (Photograph by Rimmer)*

Problems for sports teachers

In the 1950s we could have thirty-six or thirty-eight in a class, although they usually tried to avoid forty. The size of the class depended on the ability of the pupils. The more able ones were in the larger classes. In the main building of Westborough High School the classrooms were around the hall. There was no separate gymnasium so the hall was used for PE, which made for some very noisy lessons.

As far as sports were concerned, apart from netball, pupils were taken by bus to the Jones Memorial Ground, complete with all their equipment. They also went by bus to swimming lessons at the Westcliff Swimming Baths on Southend seafront, where there was an open-air swimming pool. There was also a swimming club held at the Lindisfarne Baths in Valkyrie Road after school.

The school took around 400 girls and the playground was one sloping netball court. Toilets were outside and regularly froze in the winter. Our library consisted of books placed on shelves on either side of a short corridor close to the head teacher's room. The staffroom was extremely small, but people were very friendly. Everyone had their own seat, and new members of staff tended to congregate on a hard bench at the back of the room. The head teacher, Miss Wilsher, was loved and respected by everyone.

Pamela Bissell

The Quartermaster

Both our sons were keen members of the Cubs and later Scouts. Once my wife became Akela of the Cubs I was always willing to help, but I wasn't in uniform. I acted as quartermaster and general odd-job man, but I did go to camp. We used to take the boys in a big old Dormobile with windows in the side, and that

was their transport to Belchamps. It seemed to be way out in the country, but it's been built up now.

Bill Sawford

Swimming

I learnt to swim in the swimming pool at the end of Camper Road, called Thorpe Hall Open-Air Swimming Bath on the edge of the beach at Thorpe Bay. It was very messy with rocks on the bottom and it filled up when the tide came in, but luckily it wasn't too deep. We went from school to the Westcliff Swimming Pool for lessons, but I never seemed able to swim there.

John Horsley

Kent Elms Tennis Club

My dad and granddad played tennis at Kent Elms Tennis Club. I used to walk there with my friend Martin because there was a little bit of spare land outside the one tennis court where we could play while the adults had a game of tennis. Then, as a special treat, we'd have a drink of Coke and a packet of crisps in the clubhouse.

Sometimes I played football in a field that was very close to Eastwood Primary School and near to where we lived. There were badger setts at the back of the field so we would try to see them after our games.

Mary Wigley

Tennis, cricket and a new church

It was February 1933 and I was working in the library and sometimes at the museum at Prittlewell Priory. One of my friends asked me to go along to a dance in St Luke's church hall.

Mary Wigley ready for a
ballet exam, c. 1969.

Because there was a 'flu epidemic there weren't too many people attending. That was the evening I met my wife. She attended St Luke's, so I went along too. I started playing for the church cricket club and became a member of the PCC. I also became secretary of the first Permanent Church Building Committee, as at that time services were still held in a hall. That was just before the Second World War. Revd Wardle-Harpur was the vicar in those days and he was a real character. He had previously been a curate at St Mary's and was a wonderful tennis player who got his Blue at Oxford. When he moved into the vicarage there was a large garden so he had a tennis court made so that we could form a tennis club there. We had cricket club meetings in the vestry.

Sydney Bridge

A week too late

I went in for the shot put in the Essex School Sports Competition. I reached 40ft ½ in and came second. The winner threw 41ft. The annoying part was that I went in for the sports in Southchurch Park the next week and reached 44ft, and if only I'd managed to do that the week before I'd have won the Essex

Championship and would have qualified to go in for the All England Championship as the qualifying distance was 42ft!

John Horsley

A European championship

A place I didn't know existed was a racing track for radio-controlled cars in Eastwoodbury Lane. While my husband was the mayor we were invited to the European Championships being held there. It was one of the most fantastic days of our year.

Diana Ayre

Football!

The war was over and I had, at last, left the Air Force. All my life the only thing I really wanted to do was to be a professional footballer. I was fortunate enough to be in the right place at the right time and Southend United signed me on as a professional. My ambition was achieved!

I spent four happy years playing for the team at the Southend Stadium in Sutton Road. After that I was transferred to Leeds United, by which time we had our eldest daughter, Susan. Next I played for Southampton for a few years before being moved to Cardiff City. However, I didn't want to take the family there as I thought, at nearly thirty, my football career was coming to an end. Instead we moved back to Southend and I travelled to play in Cardiff. Then I was asked to move to Brentford, but I still travelled from Southend to train and play!

Frank Dudley

Snooker

My dad won the Southend Snooker Championship in 1952 so I got interested too. I joined the leisure centre along the seafront, where the main swimming pool used to be. After about a year the snooker side closed down, but I heard that there were vacancies at St Mary's Men's Club at Prittlewell, so I applied and was accepted. I've played there ever since.

John Horsley

John Horsley in 2003.

Southend United Football Club line-up during the 1946/47 season. Frank Dudley is seated in the front row, ninth from the left out of the eleven sitting (including those in suits). (Thanks to David Goody)

A life of sport

My mother first took me to the Old Southendians' Tennis Club when I was about five. They played in Crowstone Road. Shortly after the war I visited the Westcliff Lawn Tennis Club grounds. It was like walking over a field. You could still see where it had been bombed and the ground was very rough, but then it was brought back into condition and became a tennis club once more.

I started playing badminton when I was about seven. Again I was taken by my mother, Irene Gillard, who played for the county. She used to coach at SMACS. The car showroom was at the front, but there was a badminton court at the back. Following in my mother's footsteps I played for the county too, both as a junior and later as a senior. Chalkwell Badminton Club was originally built before the war in the London Road but it was then taken over by a wholesale firm. My uncle, Ken

Frith, heard that it was up for sale after the war. After a lot of fund-raising, especially with the help of people from Leighway Badminton Club, the money was raised to buy the premises. The club moved into the new building and it is still flourishing with two courts. It is now known as Chalkwell Badminton Centre.

Although I still play tennis and badminton a new sport has entered my life. Once again that came about through my mother, who was a very keen golfer. We both belonged to Thorpe Hall Golf Club. She was the Ladies' Captain there. The clubhouse was in the original building in those days, but it has now been renovated with lovely bars and a restaurant. At first the ladies cloakroom was down in the dungeons, or so it seemed to me!

Over the last seven years I've learnt to play bowls. It isn't my favourite game, but I try to make it fun!

Sally Hall

The Leighway Badminton Club.

Cockethurst Farm

We played cricket at Cockethurst Farm, which was owned by the Fowler family. Whenever I got there I was asked to pump the water. In the kitchen there was a great big pump and the water had to be pumped up to a tank under the roof. There was also a tennis court and that was where my sister Rhoda first learnt to play. The farm was very important in our early lives.

Frank Bagnald

Game, set and match

I passed my scholarship to the grammar school but was sent to Clarks' College instead and I used to travel in by bus. Every Wednesday afternoon we went to play tennis in Priory Park, but unfortunately they only hired two courts. Only eight people could play at a time and the good players always got there early, so my friend and I didn't get on the courts until

3.45 p.m., just in time to go home. I had the idea that it would be better if we went to the cinema instead and at the cinema there was always a trailer showing what was coming the following week. That made us want to see the next film, so I didn't go to tennis again after the first few weeks.

Elvina Savill

The Roots Hall football ground

Local dignitaries founded the Southend United Football Club in 1906. Their first meeting was in the Blue Boar public house. In those days the club was in the Southern League. The first games were played on land that was later excavated for sand and later still became the Roots Hall football ground. The club moved to the greyhound stadium in Sutton Road in 1934, but when the war came the stadium was commandeered by the military.

Finals Day at Westcliff Lawn Tennis Club.

Frank Dudley in 2004.

After the war ended the club returned to the stadium, but it only had a twenty-one-year lease so, in 1955, it moved to Roots Hall for the second time.

Soon after the club moved to Roots Hall Ted Fenton was appointed as manager. He had previously been the manager of West Ham United but he had been taken ill while he was there and another manager was appointed. Luckily there was a vacancy at Southend United. Just after he arrived he rang and asked if I would go to assist him as youth manager, looking after and finding young players in their teens. I carried on with my full-time job with the council, but twice a week in the evenings and at weekends I was at the club's disposal.

That went on for about five years before Ted was replaced. At that point I didn't want to stay any longer so I left too.

Frank Dudley

The old school at Prittlewell

When I first went to school it was in the old 1865 stone building, close to St Mary's church. The infants' department was in the wing that juts out at the south east and I walked there each day from Cromwell Road, across what we called the Fête Field, the site of the old village fête. It was where Ennismore Gardens and the Drill Hall are now.

I was always very keen on football. Most of my friends were a couple of years older than I was because the school had a policy that, if you were doing well, you went up into the next form. When I was eleven I was with the fourteen-year-olds, and these older boys defended me because I was so much smaller. One day, when I was nine years old, the school team went to play Rayleigh School and I went too.

For some unknown reason I took along my football boots. Someone in the team hadn't turned up so they put me in instead – a nine-year old against fourteen-year-olds! We lost 4-1.

The headmaster, George Newland, coached me for the scholarship exam. One essay I did was a report on the football match between Southend United and Derby County in the 1925–26 season. Derby was top of the Second Division and the game was played at the Kursaal ground, which was used from 1919 until 1934. Southend United won 4-1. My father had taken me to see the match and I must admit my account of what happened was the longest essay I had ever written and the one I enjoyed most!

My links with the school continued over the years, and later I spent eighteen years as a governor.

Sydney Bridge

Sea Rangers

When I went to college I became a Cadet Ranger. Then, during the war, I took over a Guide company. When I came to Southend I was persuaded to start up a Sea Ranger crew, based at the Guide Hall in Electric Avenue. We were known as SRS Whelp. We bought a small boat called *Iona* for £8, which we moored at Westcliff and a fourteen-year-old pupil and I rowed it from the Kursaal to the mooring near Westcliff jetty in a howling gale. The tide began to ebb before we even reached the pier. I'd never rowed on the sea before and I began to wonder what I'd taken on. Unfortunately, *Iona* was smashed at the time of the Canvey flood, but later we bought a whaler with very long oars. I stayed with Sea Rangers until just before I reached retirement age and I was also the camp adviser for a number of years.

Anne Elliott

Cricket

My two great loves were always football and cricket. I honestly believe that if someone had

offered me a job playing for Southend United without payment I would have accepted. I played cricket at what is now called the County Ground in Brentwood, and while I was in Southampton I also played in the Hampshire second eleven. During my time at Eton House School I was able to coach both these sports and tried to pass on some of my enthusiasm.

Frank Dudley

Games in Eastern Close

From a very early age I went down to the beach with friends from Eastern Close, where I lived. We usually travelled by bus to the Coastguard's Station, which has now gone and been replaced by a yacht club. There were four or five children living in the close, so we used to play together. We did roller skating and played rounders, hitting balls that always seemed to land in the gardens of rather crotchety neighbours. There weren't as many cars around in the 1940s and early 50s. I also spent a lot of time playing cricket with friends at the Victory Sports Ground, which was close by and was given to the town by the Jones family.

Keith Hall

Injury!

In 1953, while I was playing for Southampton, I was badly injured so the club decided to release me. At that point my wife and I made the decision to move back to Southend and we bought a house in Central Avenue. That was where our daughter Jane was born. I started attending St Mary's church, often taking along my five-year-old daughter, Susan. Before the war I had been there as a Cub and a Scout. In those days Canon Gowing was the vicar. There have been six vicars since then, but I still belong to the church. For forty years I was on the

PCC and have been a sidesman and done many of the other jobs that came along. One day about fifteen years ago my son-in-law took me along to St Mary's Men's Club, where snooker and billiards have been played for nearly 100 years. Shortly after that I joined the committee and was chairman for some years. In fact, I had been to the club before that, because after the war Southend United footballers were invited by the committee to play there.

Frank Dudley

Family football

Coming from a large family meant that I was often taken to watch sporting events by my older brothers and sisters. I starting going to football matches when I was about seven, never dreaming in those days that I would one day marry a professional footballer.

Audrey Dudley

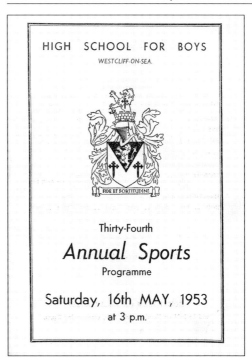

HIGH SCHOOL FOR BOYS
WESTCLIFF-ON-SEA.

FIDE ET FORTITUDINE

Thirty-Fourth

Annual Sports
Programme

Saturday, 16th MAY, 1953
at 3 p.m.

Programme for the annual Sports Day at Westcliff High School for Boys, 1953.

The long trek to church

My parents were active members of Chelmsford Avenue Congregational church, opposite the Nelson public house. Our Sunday consisted of a twenty-minute walk from Cromwell Road to the church and then back again for dinner. We had our roast meal on Saturday, because there wasn't time on Sunday. Instead we had potatoes fried in a pan, which had been left over from the day before. Then there was cold meat with sauce and afterwards Mum and I trekked back to the church for Sunday school. There were around 100 children in the primary department, and my mother was superintendent. After that we walked home again but, as both my parents were in the choir, we all trekked back again in the evening. We did that walk six times each Sunday.

Sidney Bridge

The job interview

After thirteen years as a professional footballer I realised that my playing career was ending and I had no job. At that time I was conducting a course in Southend for would-be football coaches and after one session someone suggested I enquire about vacancies at the council offices. I went for an interview in Victoria Avenue with the establishment officer for a job as a clerk in the Cemeteries and Crematorium Department. I don't think I was the first choice because they had other applicants, most of whom had been in local government for years, and I was a professional footballer.

My application had to go before a council meeting to decide if I was suitable for the job. This was for a salary of just £560 per year! When I went for the interview the chief officer was also a football fan. He sang my praises to the committee and I also had an

101

excellent reference from Canon Gowing, who was the vicar of St Mary's church, Prittlewell, for forty-three years.

I didn't get the job right away because the chairman of the committee doubted that a professional footballer could read and write! The appointment was shelved until the next month. However, I was later telephoned and told that the chairman had checked my records and discovered that I had been a navigator on Lancaster bombers during the war. Fortunately, that convinced him that I must be able to read and write and I was duly appointed. I started as a general clerk in the department and retired twenty-seven years later as the chief officer.

Frank Dudley

Golf

I took up golf after becoming a bank manager. In those days that was thought to be a suitable game for socialising and getting new business and I was given help with my subscription! At that time I was working in Chelmsford High Street, and I joined Thorpe Hall Golf Club and have remained a member ever since.

Keith Hall

Dancing feet!

I went to a school to learn ballroom dancing, and the teacher used to thump the floor in the middle of the room with a stick to give the beat. Soldiers came to her classes still wearing their hobnailed boots! We learnt to move out of the way of those boots extremely quickly.

Dances were very popular during and after the war, especially tea dances, which were held at the Kursaal, the Queen's Hotel and the Palace Hotel. The Mecca on the seafront was also well used and the Halfway House had a dance hall at the back.

Elvina Savill

Coaching at Eton House School

I had just retired from the council at the age of sixty when I was telephoned by the owner of Eton House Boys' School. He asked if I would become their football coach and PE master, so I took the job and spent the next five years very happily working there. I used to go two or three times a week to coach the lads in football and cricket. When I was sixty-five my wife and I felt it really was time to retire from my connections with football.

Frank Dudley

St Mary's Men's Club

This was established as a Charity Trust for men of the parish. I joined in 1932 when I was eighteen, carried on until the war and then returned afterwards. We played snooker and billiards. The unlicensed clubs in the town used to play for the Guinness Shield. However, when I was taking my final exams and writing my thesis I simply didn't have time to attend the club. I rejoined in 1976 and am still a member.

Sydney Bridge

Walks with my father

After the 5.30 p.m. service at St Mary's my father often took me for walks. Sometimes we went to Shoebury and than caught the train back. Shoebury Common was completely open ground then. Occasionally we went to the end of the pier where Adam Seabold had an orchestra. There was a bandstand and we sat in deckchairs to listen.

Bernard Riley

Right: *The Guinness Shield was competed for by Southend's unlicensed snooker clubs.*

Below: *St Mary's Men's Club's winning team with the Guinness Shield, c. 1986.*

9 Commerce and Trade

Late night shopping

As children we went shopping in Southend High Street after tea on Saturday evening when the shops stayed open until 9 p.m. Garons was one of the big shops at Victoria Circus. There was a restaurant and also a bakery, a greengrocery and a butchers shop. Halfway down the High Street the same family owned the Garons cinema. You could sit anywhere in the house for 1s.

At one time Sopers stood in the High Street. This was a draper's shop that had overhead wires and small containers to take the money from the assistants and then send back the change from a cash desk. Thomas's, close to Victoria Circus, had a similar system. The large jewellers in the High Street was R.A. Jones where, suspended on the wall outside and above the main door was a large clock.

When I learnt to drive, a policeman stood on a little podium at Victoria Circus. He would beckon you on when it was safe to move. Trams ran from Leigh into Southend and along Southchurch Road to Thorpe Hall Avenue where they went down to the sea. They ran on electricity with overhead cables and a rod going up from the top of the tram.

Rhoda Deane

Smells of childhood

My grandparents opened a shop in the early years of the twentieth century. It was a grocery and post office in West Road called Winn & Son and I remember the smell of disinfectant and firewood when I went into the shop. The wood was stacked up in the doorway and had a very distinctive pine smell.

There was a large bacon slicer that stood on the counter. It had a huge round blade that swished as it cut the bacon and there was a salty, briny smell. My grandmother was still around at that time but it was my Uncle Bob who did most of the work. He ran the post office that was at the back of the shop and he always seemed to be there, taking up a lot of the space because he was a big man. Looking up at him when I was small, he seemed enormous.

Behind the shop there was a storeroom, once again full of smells. Soap was stored there and later they sold greengrocery. Then there was the earthy smell of the potatoes.

The shop didn't have lino, just clean, well-worn floorboards, made to shine by endless feet.

Bill Sawford

Bargain wedding rings

When I started working in Woolworths each counter had its own assistant and many of the counters had little glass divisions to separate the products. There were two sorts of counter – island counters and side counters. The first counter on the left as you went in sold confectionery and the last counter on the left-hand side was for biscuits. There was also a

Winn & Son in West Road, c. 1910. Pictured from the left are Reg, George, their father, Bob and Lily (Bill Sawford's mother).

hardware counter and another for paint and polishes. There is still a replica Woolworths counter in London.

The hardware counter carried an enormous range of goods. On the right-hand side near the door was jewellery, which always looked very attractive. The week before a bank holiday we regularly sold at least twenty wedding rings! The cosmetics counter was extremely busy – the person in charge of the haberdashery counter had to be very knowledgeable indeed to be able to cope with all the products. We had a separate wool counter and we also sold something called Winstaino. As the name suggests, this could be stuck on the inside of windows to make them look like stained glass.

Jack Kendal

Garons

Garons was an important company in the town. The main shop was at the top of the

High Street but my father was a manager in the banqueting suite. He started working there when he was fourteen. The company did the catering for cricket matches in Chalkwell Park. They were also involved in the catering for the Coronation in 1953. Lyons Tea House was in the High Street too.

Pamela Horsley

Hamlet Court Road

There were some very nice shops in Hamlet Court Road. Havens sold beautiful china and glass, and still does. I bought my going-away suit in Alfrenes, which is also still trading. Smerdons was a large furniture shop, but it no longer exists.

It was over a shop in Hamlet Court Road that there used to be a ballroom-dancing school. I met my future husband there.

At the bottom of the road was the Queen's Hotel. This was a large, imposing building and

105

Haven's has been a popular store in Hamlet Court Road since 1901. (Thanks to Nigel Havens)

it was where we had our wedding reception. It was demolished some years ago.

Lois Holmes

The sweet-shop cottage

There used to be a small black cottage called Paste House in Eastwood Road. The lady who lived there sold sweets, five a penny – she didn't use scales. There wasn't much choice and often there were only aniseed balls. She wrapped them in newspaper cones.

Frank Bagnald

A sale bargain that wasn't!

Dixons was well known for its underwear department. I bought my first petticoat there while I was at the Municipal College. The shop was just across the road from the college

and they also had a haberdashery department. One day I bought some lace to trim another garment but when I got home I discovered that it was in a number of pieces so I took it back. I was told that, because it was a sale item, I couldn't return it. I never did get my money back!

Further down the High Street was Keddies. I was taken to tea there once by some friends and I thought the restaurant was very special. I sometimes used my one shilling lunch money in Garons while I was at the Municipal College. For that I could buy a baked jam roll and ice cream. Sometimes big ships docked at the end of the pier and my first encounter with American sailors was in Garons when they gravitated towards the group of girls I was with. Tomassi's used to sell something that was rather like a ginger sundae which was delicious.

Just off the High Street was Ravens, who were the main suppliers of school uniform. My school uniform was bought there in the

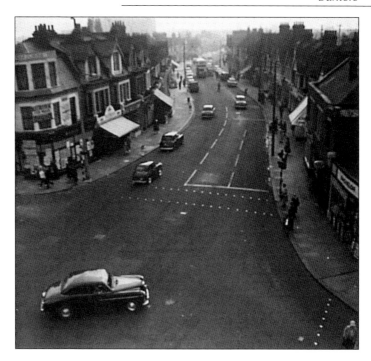

A view from Barclays Bank Flat, Hamlet Court Road, c. 1960.

first year I was at Eastwood School and then again in the third year.

Lois Holmes

The Talza Arcade

The Talza Arcade was a strange place. It was quite a labyrinth, with a number of small shops, one of which was very well known for its bacon. There was a cinema at the end of the arm that led into Southchurch Road.

Bernard Riley

The tale of a cat

My father worked in a bank. A lost cat visited several days in a row, obviously unwisely believing that this was a good place to get food. After this had been going on every day for a week or so, Dad brought it home. It was quite a clever cat because each morning he used to sit on the wall at the end of our front garden and wait for the road sweeper to come along. Then he would jump on the sweeper's trolley and get a lift to the Rayleigh Road, at Kent Elms corner. After that he would plod very slowly across this extremely busy road to go to Dorkins', the newsagents. Mrs Dorkin was very fond of cats and would always welcome him in and feed him with all her many cats. After having a lovely day with her he would plod slowly back over the road in time to come home for tea! We heard on the grapevine that bus and lorry drivers often stopped to carry him back across the Rayleigh Road.

Mary Wigley

Baxters

Baxters was a large shop at the bottom of the High Street. It had very big windows and it

Boots the Chemist occupied this imposing corner site in Southend High Street for many years.

sold clocks and all sorts of holiday gifts. Being a seaside town, Southend was always full of people searching for souvenirs to take home.

On the opposite side of the High Street was a hardware shop called Owen Wallis. It sold lawnmowers, ironmongery and if you wanted screws they had rows and rows of them.

Bill Sawford

Carnival clothes in Hamlet Court Road

When I first came to Southend in the late 1950s I worked at David Gregg's. The shop was close to Ditton Court Road in Hamlet Court Road which was a very popular shopping area. On the corner of Anerley Road there was Lavellette's, which was a beautiful gown shop. In the days when the carnival was

a major event in the Southend calendar they displayed the dresses of the queen and her court. Another clothes shop, Alfrenes, is still there and at one time they had another shop on the opposite side of the road as well.

Doreen Sawford

The High Street

Southend High Street was always a busy place in the 1950s and 1960s, and there were some large, family-run departmental stores that were very popular. At Victoria Circus was the Talza Arcade, a warren of small shops. There was a book shop that on one occasion displayed a shrunken head, which was very small, but with vast amounts of hair.

Pamela Bissell

Looking back

Southend has changed much since the 1960s and many fine old buildings have disappeared. Victoria Circus has lost the Municipal College. It might have been old fashioned in some ways, but it was a very imposing building right in the centre of the town. At that time many of the buildings in the High Street were lost, but it is still possible to look up above some of the modern façades to see living quarters from the days when families lived above their shops. Many of those windows on the higher stories are beautifully decorated. It is the same in Hamlet Court Road.

Those of us who have lived in the town for a long time still talk about Prittlewell as the village and Southend as the town. Prittlewell has been knocked about too, but luckily the church remains unchanged.

Bernard Riley

Safety first

The knives used to cut all the meats in David Gregg's stores were extremely sharp and inevitably there were accidents from time to time. Tongues arrived in tins and it was a real job to get them out. The worst cut I ever had was when I was carving one of those. The knife slipped and sliced my thumb. There were never any special plasters in those days, as there are now – at that time you just had to sort yourself out as best you could.

Doreen Sawford

Working at Keddies

Early in the 1950s I became secretary to Maitland Keddie, the managing director of the High Street store. It was fascinating to see the workings of a large departmental store from the inside. The outside of Selfridges in London had been the inspiration for the shopfront.

Selfridges inspired the shopfront of Keddies, now divided into smaller shops.

There was plenty of professional rivalry between Keddies and the other large family firm in the town, Dixons. Once, by mistake, we were sent the printer's proof of their advertisement for the following week, so this was studied with interest and everything was then reduced in our store by one farthing! I was on one occasion sent along to Dixons to check on how many were in the audience for the mannequin show.

Elvina Savill

David Gregg's

This was an old-type provisions and grocery shop. The floor was of black and white tiles and to clean it they put down sawdust. This would never be allowed today. The left-hand side of the shop as you went through the door was for groceries. In the middle at the back was the cashier and then, as you came down the right-hand side, butter and cheeses were sold. The last thing you reached was the ham, close to the door. This was always hand carved.

When I first arrived the Westcliff shop seemed tiny. It was a unique store in its way and they sold their own Scotch cake. This was a large slab of cake and the customer could have a piece cut off for 2s. Ham was about 2s a quarter.

Eighty-pound New Zealand cheeses were available and they had to be cut on the cheese board with a wire. You would cut them in half and then quarters, and then the middle piece was removed with a boning knife. That was the piece everyone wanted because it didn't have any rind. Then all the pieces were cut into wedges. Often customers wanted you to start cutting a new cheese so they could have a middle piece.

Doreen Sawford

The Blue Boar

In the 1930s the chef of the Blue Boar in Victoria Avenue always seemed to have an enormous joint and he carved the meat in front of the customers. The counter was imposing because it was raised up on a platform and the chef looked down on his customers as he carved his enormous hunk of meat with a great carving knife.

Jack Kendall

Doreen and Bill Sawford in 2003.

Sally Hall with Mrs Smerdon of the large furniture store in Hamlet Court Road.

Victoria Avenue

When I first came to Southend, large houses lined Victoria Avenue, and where the Churchill Gardens are now, the lady who lived there used to breed dogs. One of my friends bought a boxer puppy from her. The garden had a huge sunken area that has now become the centre of the beautiful memorial gardens. There was a little group of shops opposite the Blue Boar, close to St Mary's church, which included a hairdresser's shop and a draper's called Sopers.

Pamela Bissell

Like a stately home!

Brightwell's had a massive staircase at the back of the shop. It was like being in a stately home with the stairs splitting halfway up and going in opposite directions to the next floor. The walls were lined with dark wood, which made the shop feel very special. Among other things they sold underwear, including corsets that had bones and were kept together with laces. I used to go there sometimes with my grandmother.

On the other side of the High Street there was Tomassi's. The restaurant still exists but has now moved to the other side of the road. They sold amazing milkshakes and we often went there with our friends as teenagers. Cotgroves' was well known for its fish and chips, and at one time we went there to celebrate New Year.

Newbury's in Hamlet Court Road was a little baker's shop that sold the most delicious cakes. Upstairs was a café and we would be taken there by my grandmother. To have a Charlotte Russe was a very special treat. Further up the road there was Smerdons, a very smart furniture shop. Havens, a very large shop selling china and other goods, is still a feature of the road.

Right at the bottom of Hamlet Court Road was the Queen's Hotel. We often went there to ballroom dances.

Sally Hall

Visiting Grandma

One day during the war we visited Southend from Kent by going via Liverpool Street. I was with my mum and sister and there seemed to be soldiers everywhere. We came through to Westcliff and then walked up Hamlet Court Road to reach my grandmother's shop in West Road. It was on the corner of Silverdale Avenue. If you went all the way to Southend there were problems because it was a restricted area. When we travelled we always had to have our gas masks.

Bill Sawford

Learning the ropes in a grocery store

When you first went to work for David Gregg's you started on the left-hand grocery side and you had to deal with the biscuits, sugar and the jams. Then you moved to the other side of the shop where you learnt to pat the butter and weigh the lard. Next you had to be able to cut and skin the cheese, because it always came in wrapped in muslin-like cloths. It was really hard work pulling the skin off.

You also had to learn to bone a side of bacon and roll the joints. This needed a very sharp knife as all the individual bones had to be removed. The bacon was then sliced on the cutting machine. Finally, after working your way round the store, you reached the ham counter. Here you had to be able to skin the hams and hand carve them. This again was done with a very sharp knife that was usually sharpened by one of the men.

As food became more plentiful the shop began to change. At one time chickens would come in and then hang in the shop. Then Buxted chickens arrived and they were much cheaper than the ones previously sold. The window would then be filled with the chick-

ens. There had been a Gregg's in Southend High Street, and when the area was redeveloped in the 1960s they moved and opened a self-service shop.

David Gregg's was a good company to work for. In the past you would never see a Gregg's where there was a Sainsbury's. They had an agreement when they first opened, but in later years the agreement lapsed.

I worked for David Gregg's in Hamlet Court Road from 1958 until 1965 and at the end of that time, although there were many changes, I was still hand carving ham. The really major changes came in the 1970s with the growth of supermarkets.

Doreen Sawford

Working for Dixons

For ten years I worked in the fashion department of Dixons at Victoria Circus, and Mr John Dixon was in charge. His brother Eric worked for Marconi, but when the bridge was built across Queens Road to the other part of the shop, he helped with the construction. He had a standby generator put on the roof in case of power cuts. When there were sales all the family members came in and worked behind the counters. On Friday night Mr John always stayed behind in his office so that anyone with problems, either at work or home, could go and talk to him. That was the sort of company Dixons was.

Babs Haywood

Prittlewell shops

There was a Co-op shop opposite the Blue Boar in Victoria Avenue. This was useful as it was close to St Mary's church. Another important shop for me was Liddiard's, next door to the church hall. Although it was well known as a pram shop, it also sold bikes. My

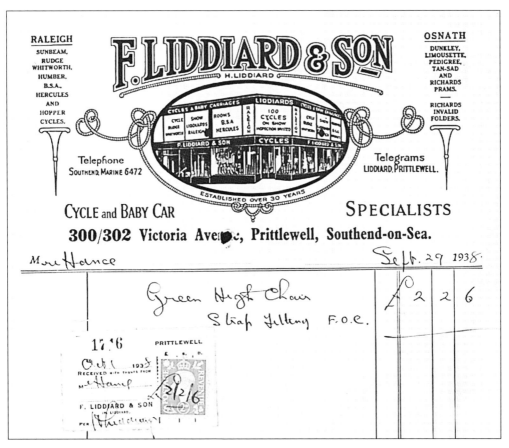

A 1938 receipt for a high chair from Liddiard's store, Prittlewell.

first green Raleigh Lentern sports bike with drop handlebars came from that shop. I'd been gazing longingly at it for ages and I think I finally got it for passing my Eleven Plus exam.

Keith Hall

Foil to foil the Germans

My great-grandfather started a factory where tin foil was manufactured. Whenever I went to the factory as a child I was quite over-whelmed by the large machinery, the fumes from the dyes and the noise, but it was a very exciting place. It was called W.G. Frith's Co.

Ltd and was close to the Prittlewell Station.

Aluminium foil was used during the war to disturb radar systems. It was cut into thin strips and dropped from planes. It was often known as 'glitter'. For a time the firm moved to Shrewsbury, but later returned. It was very much a family business because all my uncles and cousins worked there.

After the war the coloured foil was used for sweet and chocolate biscuit wrappers. In 1998 it left the control of the family when it was sold and the name changed to Frith's Flexible Packaging.

Sally Hall

Shops at Jones' Corner, Eastwood, probably in the late 1920s.

A question of blinds

The manager of the Westcliff branch of David Gregg's was quite paranoid about the blinds. They were black ones that could be pulled down. He insisted that they must be down if there was the slightest sign of sunshine, so the shop always appeared to be closed. I found this very strange after being in a larger shop where everything was always open and light.

An area inspector visited from time to time. He always went mad about the blinds. Then, on one occasion, he came to take over when our manager went on holiday. He decided he wouldn't have the windows covered by blinds again so he cut the cords! When the manager returned he was not amused. Not long after that he was replaced.

Doreen Sawford

Cold feet!

My father worked as a tailor in Aldgate. He made ladies' suits and coats. I went to work with him, but I didn't like it so I left and tried millinery and later dressmaking. After that I went to Woolworths in Hamlet Court Road. I enjoyed that, but later I moved to British Home Stores in Southend High Street. At first I sold make-up, but then I moved to records. We celebrated my twenty-first birthday upstairs in the shop.

Later I worked at Nats in the Talza Arcade. We sold lingerie and stockings. At one point I had trouble with my feet. That was because we had lino on the floor and the three doors were always kept open so it was very cold. I ended up in hospital and had to have an operation.

Jean Lesser

10 A Town of Many Parts

A close-knit Leigh family

My father started as a cockle fisherman before the age of fifteen because he was working for his brothers. Then he went into partnership with one of his brothers. Father was one of twelve children. My grandparents were both Osbornes, although they were not related. My great-grandparents had owned the Kings Head, which stood where Leigh Station was later built, but when the railway came through, the pub was destroyed. They were offered the Carlton in The Broadway, but they felt they were too old to take on a new pub of that size, so instead they went to the Woodcutters, close to Belfairs.

Father was the middle of the twelve children, so I grew up believing that some of my cousins were aunts and uncles. Because of the size of the family we didn't really need to make friends outside the family circle. In fact, as a child, I can't remember anyone ever coming into the house who wasn't a relative.

There were three families of Osbornes that sometimes intermarried. In one of the electoral rolls of the 1800s there was one John Osborne married to Mary Osborne. Three doors away there was another John Osborne married to Sarah Osborne and another three doors away there was yet another John Osborne married to Sarah Osborne. They all seemed to use the same names for their children so many nicknames were used. The Barnard side of the family were buried in St Clement's churchyard, although more recently Leigh Cemetery has been used. When our banns were called the rector, Revd Burrdock of St Margaret's, said he could trace our family back to King Henry VIII's time.

Elvina Savill

The Townswomen's Guild in Eastwood

I was the first chairman of the Eastwood Townswomen's Guild in 1947–48 and we often went to Cockethurst Farmhouse for our committee meetings. We formed the Guild because we felt there was a real need as at that time many of the women living on the Devonshire Estate were young and had small children. If we held our meetings in the evening then the husbands could babysit while the mothers had some time out. We held two meetings each month: one was a business meeting and one was for pleasure. This worked really well and the Guild has flourished ever since.

The Devonshire Estate went through from the Arterial Road to Snakes Lane. A tennis club was also built on the estate with a clubhouse and just one court and for many years the club was run by Doreen McClellan and John Perkins.

Rhoda Deane

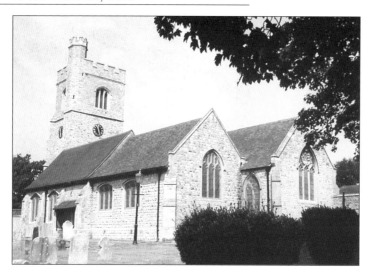

St Clement's church, Leigh.

Past chairmen of Eastwood Evening Townswomen's Guild at their twenty-first birthday party in 1970. From left to right: Edna Starr, Sybil Spanton, Irene Dennis, Maureen Ollett, Rhoda Sandford and Rhoda Deane (Shanahan). (Thanks to Echo Newspapers)

Pier disasters

I photographed three major pier disasters. The first was the devastating fire at the pier head. The second was when a ship went through the middle of the pier and the third was when the bowling lanes at the shore end burnt down.

When the ship went through the pier I was only able to photograph the gap; the boat had gone by the time I arrived. The photographs of the burning of the bowling lanes happened because I was telephoned by the Evening Echo newspaper. I received an early morning call at home in Brentwood and I rushed down to Southend and flew off to take the pictures. Although the fire was very intense, from a photographer's point of view, it was less spectacular than the fire at the end of the pier.

Edward Clack

The synagogue

My parents joined the synagogue in Ceylon Road. When we were sixteen we had our own club. We used to have a Sunday school and we decided to put on a concert and play. We charged people to come and see it and all the money went to buy Hebrew books and other things for the synagogue. Dad made my clothes and my friend Betty and I did a tango. I loved it. I think performing was in the blood, as my father was on the stage at one time and he could have gone to America with Charlie Chaplin, but my grandfather wouldn't let him go. He wanted him to stay and be a tailor.

Jean Lesser

Moving to Prittlewell

In the early 1960s we moved from Leigh to North Crescent in Prittlewell. Behind our bungalow were the Kent and Essex Farmers' Nurseries. They grew vegetables. We could see for miles from our back garden, and the sky filled three-quarters of the view, because everywhere was so open. Now the land has been taken over by Tesco and the Royal Bank of Scotland. There is also a small park and fortunately some of the park land adjoins my bungalow.

Pamela Bissell

Eastwood cottages

There were several small thatched cottages in Eastwoodbury Lane. Two were known as Nos 1 and 2 Pillar Box Cottages because there was a pillar box outside. Two belonged to the Fowler family and were used by their farm workers, and there were also some that were known as the Workhouse Cottages. That must have been where the workhouse was before the Rochford Workhouse was built.

Jean Lesser in 2003.

Mrs Costin lived in one of the cottages. Her daughter was killed by a bus just before one Christmas, and her room in the cottage was never altered from the morning she left to go to school. In the early 1960s the cottages were burnt down.

Frank Bagnald

Life at the YWCA

On arrival in Southend the first priority was to find somewhere to live. We came searching a week before the start of the new school year. The YWCA, which was on the top of the cliffs near the bandstand, offered the only suitable accommodation. This meant sharing a bedroom with four other people. As my bed was in the corner I had to climb over everyone else to reach it! The only ventilation was a large French door and you either slept with it open and shivered or shut and stewed.

117

Eastwood Church is mentioned in Domesday Book.

The hostel was crowded and there was only one bathroom, and we all needed to wash at the same time in the morning. Fortunately, I discovered a cupboard upstairs with a large butler's sink, one cold tap and no plug – not ideal, but I used it.

Anne Elliott

Becoming mayor of Southend

There were sixteen aldermen and forty-eight councillors for the sixteen wards in Southend when I joined the council. I served for sixteen years as a councillor before becoming deputy mayor in 1990. That was a time of learning the ropes before becoming mayor. In 1991 I became mayor in my own right, and during that exciting year I attended approximately 500 different events. One very memorable occasion was the Mayor Making Ceremony,

which was the official start of my year of office. It took place in the Council Chamber and I received the Chain of Office.

One of the great things about being mayor was having the opportunity to use Porters, a beautiful house originally built in 1492. American visitors loved to hear that they were visiting a house built when Christopher Columbus was setting out for America. People from all walks of life visited the house, including many school children and once a group came from Chernobyl. One of my council colleagues prepared a speech for me in Russian. I hope they understood!

Geoffrey Ayre

New gates for Priory Park

My father loved Southend and its history. During his final year at the London Road

Right: *Anne Elliott in 2003.*

Below: *Priory Park Gates, given to the town by R.A. Jones.*

Boys' School be became head boy. He was asked to go to Priory Park when R.A. Jones presented the gates to the town. He always felt really protective towards the park and he wrote many letters to the papers when suggestions were made that a section of the park should be used for road widening. He believed passionately that the park was given to the people of Southend and should be preserved for their use. He was always very proud of the town.

Lois Holmes

An unusual landlady

After leaving the YWCA we moved to Prittlewell Chase. Our new landlady was extremely eccentric – she never put the light on, but sat in her sitting room by the light of the street lamp. In the eighteen months we were there she only had three fires and those were because her small granddaughter came to visit. At 6 p.m. every night she went out to visit a friend and returned at ten when she hurried upstairs and got ready for bed, again using the street light. The only hot water we had, apart from what we boiled in the kettle, was on Monday. That was when we had to do our washing and have a bath. After that the boiler went out until the following Monday. Her constant rebuke was 'Forgetfulness lays the paving stones to hell!' I guess we made quite a path.

Anne Elliott

The Eastwood Memorial Hall

There was a farm next door to the old Eastwood School that was run by a Mr Collingwood. He kept cows and he was also very keen on whist. I joined the players one Christmas. Further along the road was the Eastwood Memorial Hall, and my father was

one of the trustees when it was first built. One of the founders of the hall was Mr Kotch, a German. He lived in Rochford Road, later renamed Whitehouse Road. He was a very clever man, and if he wanted something then he made it.

Rochford Corner at Eastwood used to be known as Munns' Corner after a Mr Munns who ran a market garden there.

Frank Bagnald

Elections

Lord and Lady Iveigh both at different times served as MPs for Southend. Later, their son-in-law, Henry Channon, took the seat. He didn't drive, so on one occasion I drove him throughout the election campaign. He had his own chauffeur at home but during the election period he stayed at the Palace Hotel and I took over the driving.

Rhoda Deane

Life in Royal Terrace

We moved from Prittlewell Chase to Royal Terrace, and the accommodation was a bed-sit on the west corner of the terrace. Everything had been dyed red, and all the reds were of different shades depending on the fabric. The room was large and it had a small, screened washbasin and whenever the wind blew the window frames rocked. All the cooking was done in a tiny, shared kitchen with two sinks side by side and three gas stoves. A pilot, an insurance agent and Mr Baker, who had the front flat, occupied the rest of our floor. We all shared the bathroom which had an ancient Ascot-type water heater and the bath. The water was never warmer than tepid! The pilot always seemed to be cooking and the landlady came in when we were out and cooked kippers on our

Royal Terrace, where the princesses Caroline and Charlotte once stayed.

stove, leaving behind a greasy pan and a very strong smell!

Anne Elliott

A chapter of coincidences

Quite by chance I took the only aerial photographs of the pier head burning. It happened like this. Among my other duties at the airport I flight-tested aeroplanes. I had a test to do on a twin-engined Piper Apache. The engineers were late delivering it for testing and it was finally handed over at around six in the evening.

I took off and went towards Clacton, with someone else with me to make notes, but I found a fault and had to abandon the test and return to Southend Airport. As I came in I saw a huge column of smoke rising into the sky from somewhere in Southend. After landing I gathered up my camera and took off in a Piper Cherokee and decided to see what was happening.

The sight that greeted me was one of the most awe-inspiring I had ever seen. The end of the pier was a raging inferno. The tide was out and there were two fireboats near by, but they couldn't get in close enough to be of much use.

But for the test flight being delayed I would have left for home in Brentwood before news of the fire came in. As it happened everything was absolutely perfect that night for photography. The ambient light was beginning to fail but there was just enough to illuminate the background which emphasised the brilliant flames rising into the darkening sky. Those

An amazing aerial photograph of the pier head burning. (Copyright Edward Clack)

photographs were sold to newspapers all over the country and the world. They are still displayed at the end of the pier.

Edward Clack

Arrival in Eastwood

I married in 1959 and after a brief spell in Ilford we decided to move further down the railway line. We ended up on a new estate in Eastwood. At that time many people still thought of Eastwood as the heart of the country and it was usually referred to as 'the village'. I thought it was fantastic because I could see fields out of the upstairs window.

As a newcomer I wanted to meet new people. One of my neighbours, Joan Sammons, took me to a meeting of the Townswomen's Guild in the local Memorial Hall. Leaflets had been put around to encourage younger members from the new estates. We both joined. Some time after that we were late arriving for one meeting and were ushered into the front row. That was the night of nominations for the new committee and by the end of the evening we were both nominated and shortly afterwards elected. In a way that evening changed my life.

Maureen Ollett

Housing problems

At the end of the war there were severe housing problems. We put our names down on the housing list and were told to wait and, in the meantime, try to find something ourselves. We didn't hear any more. Luckily my father and his brother were small-time builders and there was a vacant plot in Crowborough Road. They built two houses and I took one and my uncle had the other. That was in 1947. We moved in and have stayed ever since.

Bernard Riley

Members of Eastwood Evening TWG whist group, 1981.

Married to the mayor

One of the proudest moments of my life came when I was in the Council Chamber as my husband was made mayor. After Geoffrey was chained so was I. The mayoress' chain is really wonderful with its setting of sapphires, rubies and diamonds. The chains were always carried separately in a special case in the boot of the car when we travelled away from town. We put them on just before reaching our destination. On one occasion we went to Castle Hedingham. On the way we stopped for a coffee in a pub and afterwards we were chained in the car park, much to the amusement of the local residents.

Before the mayoral year started I spent hours with my friends sewing little eyes on our clothes so the chains could be hooked on. In that way our clothes weren't damaged and the chains sat properly. This was essential because they are extremely heavy.

Clothes were obviously important. We were given a grant, but I really needed a new wardrobe. I did a lot of mixing and matching and bought clothes that could be used in different ways.

Diana Ayre

Spy in the Sky

I've often given illustrated talks to groups, leaving a time for questions at the end. One day a lady asked why I didn't put my photographs and words together and make a book. That triggered the writing of *Spy in the Sky*, which included photographs of Southend and the burning pier head. *Spy in the Sky* was a nickname I picked up when I was a reconnaissance photographer at RAF Habbaniyah, close to Baghdad. The book sold 16,000 copies. Since then I have completed other books on the area. There is one called *The Beauty of Flight*, and for that I travelled around the country. Then there is *In Defence of Essex*.

This isn't to do with the war but shows what a beautiful place our county is, so the title is really a play on words. The most recent one is about the River Blackwater and is called *Tales from the River* and I have also edited and put together a book about Hullbridge which is called *Paths of Former Time*.

Edward Clack

The Canvey floods

The Townswomen's Guild always had strong music and drama groups. Our choir entered the Leigh Music Festival each year and there was also a very popular drama festival. Miss Nevard conducted the choir. Some members wanted lighter music at one point, as probably it was all rather highbrow. In February 1953 the choir was supposed to be entertaining at Haig Hall, but they couldn't because the hall had been taken over for the victims of the Canvey floods.

Maureen Ollett

Chains

When the town became a borough in 1892 the first mayor, Thomas Dowsett, bought the chain and badge and presented them to the town. The mayoress' chain goes back to about 1932 when the mayor at that time, Robert Tweedy Smith, bought the mayoress' chain (at the urging of his wife!).

During the Southend Air Display we were invited by the RAF to lunch and I was wearing my chain. After we had eaten I thought I would go and watch some of the displays, but the assistant mace-bearer, who was accompanying us that day, couldn't be found. However, I was with officers so I thought all was well. Unfortunately, I was in real trouble when I got back for going off wearing the chain and without a proper guard. In my innocence I thought I was perfectly safe being surrounded by members of the armed forces of the Crown!

Our day ended with a helicopter trip. That time the chains were removed first. No more risks were being taken!

Diana Ayre

Edward Clack with his plane, his camera and his books!

Well and truly stuck

I took part in Southend Carnival as a member of the Barking and Dagenham carnival court. Carnival queens and their attendants were expected to pose on decorated floats, smiling and waving to the crowds. As the procession made its way slowly along the Esplanade the top part of our elaborately festooned float hit the lower part of the pier bridge. We were well and truly stuck! The whole procession ground to a halt.

There were no police or carnival marshals around so my father, who just happened to be standing close to the bridge, risked life and limb by climbing onto the vehicle in an attempt to dislodge the offending bar. Hanging perilously on the back of the lorry he finally managed it, although it took a good ten minutes. As he clambered down, a great cheer went up and it was his photograph that appeared next day in the *Southend Standard*!

Sylvia Kent

Sylvia Kent won the Queen of Queens competition in Southend carnival in 1963.

Bob Winn, a character to remember

My uncle, Bob Winn, was quite a character. He was the youngest of four children, and at one time he had a yacht. It was quite a big one and we went out on it sometimes. There is a family story that he took the boat out to go to Dunkirk to rescue troops, but unfortunately he didn't make it because the boat broke down on the way.

He had an orchard close to Hobblythick Lane where he grew apples, plums and gooseberries and he also kept bees. He rode a trade bike to get there. There was a machine to mix the honey but it wasn't very efficient because there was always a sticky mess after it had been used. He loved the history of churches.

After my grandmother died he started decorating every room at once in the flat over the shop and post office. He installed a very peculiar bath under the sink unit. The unit swivelled and it must have been an awful job to get in because the bath was small and he was large. His bedroom was also unusual as it was jam-packed with memorabilia and books.

He was a very kind and well-respected man and everyone had a good word to say for him. Later he opened another post office in West Street and he used to travel between the two offices by bike.

Bill Sawford

Ready for the tip

The mayor's chair was originally made from wood taken from the old pier. When the new

125

civic centre buildings were ready for occupation the old council chambers in Clarence Street were emptied. Someone passing happened to notice that the skip outside the building contained a rather ornate chair. Luckily he realised that this was something rather special. Apparently someone had decided that the old mayor's chair was unsuitable for the new building. Fortunately it was rescued and is once more in use.

Diana Ayre

The Oakwood Pumping Station

My grandfather, Charlie Claydon, worked at the pumping station in Eastwood. It was called the Oakwood Pumping Station and it pumped the water that came in from Maldon. Years later the Oakwood pub was built close by.

Babs Haywood

Returning officer in plaster

During my year of office as mayor there was a General Election. The mayor acts as returning officer at that time. Unfortunately I had ruptured a tendon in my leg so I was walking on crutches. I awaited the result in my office in the civic centre and later I had to go out to make the announcement. This was to be televised, which is not the time you want to have your leg in plaster!

Geoffrey Ayre

An invitation to Buckingham Palace

We were invited to Buckingham Palace as the official representatives of the town during Geoffrey's mayoral year. We went up very early and had a picnic lunch, complete with champagne, in Green Park and then we completed our dressing before setting out for the palace. This is one time when the mayor does not wear his chain. We queued to go in and our names were checked on a list. It was a very hot day. We saw the Royal Family from a distance and our iced coffee was served in incredibly small cups!

Diana Ayre

Growing up in a Jewish family

On the Day of Atonement we all had to fast. We were told by our mother to lay the table, but we were warned not to eat a crumb, so I watched my sister Kitty and she watched me! We laid the table with pickled herring and other special food and afterwards we took an

The gravestone of Jean Lesser's father.

Yachts preparing to sail at Thorpe Bay.

orange and a piece of cake and hid them in our bags when we went back to the synagogue. Then, as soon as we heard the shofar blown to end the fast, we ran outside and ate our hidden food. I can't fast any more now because of my age.

Passover is also important for Jewish families. For our special meal Dad sat at the head of the table. Mum was at the foot and Kitty and I sat on either side. At the beginning we had a soup plate with salt water and one egg in it. Then we had soup, chicken and afterwards prunes. A piece of unleavened bread was hidden by my dad and at one point, when the angel was supposed to come in, Dad shook the table, which scared my sister. We had a special plate with bitter herbs, onion and a burnt egg which meant that while there's life there's death. The meal took about two hours.

On the Sabbath my mother put a shawl over her head and said prayers over the candles. Then we had another special meal.

Now I go to the Day Centre at the synagogue and we sometimes go by coach to the Jewish Cemetery and put a stone on our parents' graves to show that we've been there.

Jean Lesser

Learning about Southend

I thoroughly enjoyed my time as mayor and I learnt an enormous amount about Southend. It is an extremely charitable town. Money was raised to buy equipment for the hospital and for many other charities.

Southend parks are superb, and for the last ten years the town has been represented at the Chelsea Flower Show. Medals have been won every year, with two golds in 2002 and 2003.

Geoffrey Ayre

Other local titles published by Tempus

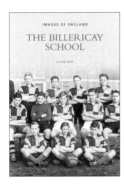

The Billericay School
SYLVIA KENT

The creation of the Billericay School in May 1937 as the town's first senior school marked the beginning of an exciting era for the town and its families. This compilation of over 200 images and detailed information is drawn from past and present pupils and school staff along with contributions from Billericay residents. It is sure to appeal to anyone with an interest in the history of the Billericay School as well as the town.
0 7524 3083 1

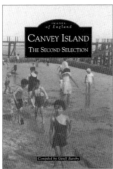

Canvey Island The Second Selection
GEOFF BARSBY

In this book the Canvey Island of the past has been evocatively recreated using over 200 photographs, postcards and engravings documents. From the time pioneering engineer Brigadier-General R.B. Colvin built the bridge that connected Canvey Islanders to their neighbour Benfleet, to the beginnings of the resort that flourished in the heyday of the 1950s, each image will delight all those who have ever known this area.
0 7524 2260 X

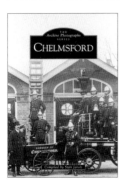

Chelmsford
STAN JARVIS

From the nineteenth century, new factories and workshops attracted large numbers of people to Chelmsford and the subsequent development began to shape the town we see today. Using images from the Spalding photographic collection, and the collections of author Stan Jarvis and local photographer Peter Russell, this memorable book serves as a fascinating record of those times and will prove irresistible to all those who know Chelmsford.
0 7524 0734 1

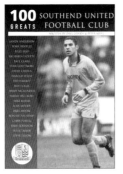

Southend United Football Club 100 Greats
DAVE GOODY AND PETER MILES

Compiled by two lifelong supporters, this volume salutes the 100 greatest names in the club's long history. Those selected include stalwarts noted for their longevity and record breaking, such as Sandy Anderson, Alan Moody, Billy Best and Roy Hollis. Gifted players who spent only a short time at Southend but contributed much to the folklore of the club, like Stan Collymore, also make the top 100. Each player is profiled with detailed biographical and statistical records.
0 7524 2177 8

If you are interested in purchasing other books published by Tempus, or in case you have difficulty finding any Tempus books in your local bookshop, you can also place orders directly through our website

www.tempus-publishing.com

or from   **BOOKPOST**, Freepost, PO Box 29, Douglas, Isle of Man, IM99 1BQ
tel 01624 836000   email bookshop@enterprise.net